THE UNIVERSITY OF NORTH CAROLINA
SOCIAL STUDY SERIES

I0132198

PUBLIC POOR RELIEF
IN NORTH CAROLINA

THE UNIVERSITY OF NORTH CAROLINA
SOCIAL STUDY SERIES

THE UNIVERSITY OF NORTH CAROLINA PRESS
CHAPEL HILL, N. C.

THE BAKER AND TAYLOR CO.
NEW YORK

OXFORD UNIVERSITY PRESS
LONDON

MARUZEN-KABUSHIKI-KAISHA
TOKYO

1. The Vance County Hospital

This institution has been converted from a county home into a regular hospital for the poor, recognized by the Duke Foundation. There is a ward for the aged poor.

PUBLIC POOR RELIEF IN NORTH CAROLINA

BY

Roy M. Brown

*Research Associate in the Institute
for Research in Social Science
University of North Carolina*

CHAPEL HILL
THE UNIVERSITY OF NORTH CAROLINA PRESS
1928

PRINTED IN THE UNITED STATES OF AMERICA
BY EDWARDS & BROUGHTON COMPANY, RALEIGH, N. C.

THIS BOOK WAS DIGITALLY PRINTED.

PREFACE

THE plan for this volume began with the preparation for the State Board of Charities and Public Welfare of a bulletin on poor relief in North Carolina, published early in 1925. From this study and other experience in my work with the State Board, it became evident that a brief analysis of the development of public poor relief in the state from colonial times to the present would make a needed addition to our knowledge and picture in the field of public welfare. It is, therefore, with pleasure that I am able to present such a study through the Institute for Research in Social Science at the University of North Carolina. It is hoped that this volume may fit in with others of the University Social Study Series, especially with those on social work and public welfare, and that it may be followed by similar volumes on still other aspects of the subject.

In the course of the preparation of the volume I have become indebted to a number of people, and especially to Professor J. F. Steiner for many helpful suggestions in the organization of the material and the preparation of the manuscript; to Mr. George B. Logan, Mr. R. B. House, and Professor W. B. Sanders for reading and criticizing the manuscript; to Mrs. Kate Burr Johnson, state commissioner of public welfare, for permitting the freest use of material in her office; to Dr. Guion Griffis Johnson for generously placing at my disposal certain material gathered for her social history of North Carolina; to Dr. E. C. Branson for valuable material on

Orange County; to Miss Katherine Jocher, assistant
director of the Institute for Research in Social Science
at the University of North Carolina, for many courtesies
in the preparation of the manuscript; and to Dr. H. W.
Odum for continued interest and help from the date of
the initial suggestion of the possibility of such a volume
through its publication.

R. M. B.

CHAPEL HILL
  February, 1928

CONTENTS

ILLUSTRATIONS

PUBLIC POOR RELIEF
IN NORTH CAROLINA

CHAPTER I

THE ENGLISH BACKGROUND

THE first squatter who raised his cabin in the wilderness
that was to be North Carolina may have dreamed of a
land where there would be a minimum of government,
where he might escape the tyranny of English customs.
But he was an Englishman. And when it was necessary
for him to adopt customs and laws for his own guidance,
or when such customs and laws were imposed upon him,
they were the customs and laws of England. The principles and practices of poor relief which came into use
in North Carolina had their beginnings in the early days
of England, and their development must be traced in
English history. For an understanding of the adaptation
and development of those principles and practices here,
some knowledge of the evolution of the English Poor
Law is, therefore, indispensable. A brief summary of
that evolution for this reason seems a desirable introduction to the present study of the development and administration of poor relief in North Carolina.

The English in the early years of their history in
Great Britain lived for the most part in neighborhoods
or communities, each, as compared with the modern
community, a unit within itself. There was little
mobility.[1] One belonged in a certain place. Quite naturally the community came to be considered as having
some responsibility for its members. And quite as

[1] S. A. Queen, *Social Work in the Light of History*, p. 166.

naturally, also, the customs which grew out of this feeling of responsibility became the law of the land. Thus, early in the tenth century the law required that every peasant who had no home of his own should live with some householder if he would be regarded as a member of the community and entitled to protection.[2] By the early years of the next century each householder was held responsible for every member of his household, whether free or bond, and for the stranger within his gates.[3]

Near the middle of the fourteenth century the great plague swept over England. Many laborers died. Those who survived felt themselves in position to demand higher wages. Parliament, composed largely of landlords, on the other hand, was anxious to keep the laborers in subjection. A law accordingly was enacted which not only required that every laborer under sixty years of age should continue to labor in his accustomed place at the wage accustomed to be given, but forbade the asking of alms by "valiant beggars" or the giving of alms to such beggars, and classed one who stood out for higher wages with the professional beggar.[4] Toward the close of the century, in an attempt further to fix by law the residence of the laborer, it was enacted that no servant or laborer should depart from the "hundred, rape, or wapentake" where he was dwelling, to work or dwell elsewhere, or on any other pretense, without an official letter explaining the cause of his going. If any servant

[2] Sir George Nicholls, *History of the English Poor Law*, I, 13.

[3] *Ibid.*, p. 14.

[4] Queen, *op. cit.*, p. 168.

or laborer should be found in any city or borough or elsewhere than his place of residence, he should "be taken and put in the stocks, and kept until he found surety to return to his service, or to serve and labor in the town from whence he came."[5] Beggars "impotent to serve" must abide in the cities and towns where they were dwelling at the time of the proclamation of the statute.[6] A little later one's place of residence was somewhat more definitely defined as the hundred in which he last dwelt or was best known or was born.[7]

Thus gradually what has become known as the law of legal settlement took form until under Elizabeth the place of birth, if that was known, otherwise the parish in which the person last dwelt for one year, was declared his place of settlement.[8] Finally the justices of the peace were empowered, upon complaint of the church wardens or overseers of the poor, to remove to the place of his legal residence any person likely to become chargeable to the parish.[9]

Laws relating to legal settlement, treated first here because of their earlier beginnings, became finally supplementary to the general poor law. It was not until the last quarter of the fourteenth century that the English law definitely recognized the impotent poor as a distinct class. It was then provided that "beggars impotent to serve" should abide in the cities and towns where they

---

[5] Nicholls, *op. cit.*, I, 55; 12 Richard II, 1388.

[6] Queen, *op. cit.*, p. 169.

[7] 11 Henry VII, c. 2, 1495.

[9] 39 Elizabeth, c. 4, 1597-98.

[8] "Settlement Act," 14 Charles II, c. 12, 1662.

were dwelling at the time of the proclamation of the statute, but that if the people of such cities and towns would not, or might not, "suffice to find them," they might within forty days withdraw to other towns within the "hundred, rape, or wapentake," or to the towns where they were born and there abide during the remainder of their lives.[10] The next step was to fix more precisely who might beg by providing for a census of the poor and for the licensing of such of the poor as in the opinion of local officials should be permitted to beg within certain definite limits.[11] So far the obligation of the community to relieve the suffering of the poor had been implied but not clearly defined. Provision was now made that the impotent poor should be so relieved by voluntary alms, gathered through the agency of the church, that none should be compelled to beg; that the poor returned to their place of settlement should be "most charitably" received; and that "sturdy vagabonds and valiant beggars" should be set to labor to earn their own living.[12] There was laid down the important principle that none should "go openly begging,"[13] and the scarcely less important corollary that no one might give to the relief of the poor except through the agencies established by law.[14]

Prior to the reign of Henry VIII, the relief of the poor to a very large extent had been undertaken by the church. The ideal involving the duty of aiding the poor

[10] 12 Richard II, 1388.

[11] 22 Henry VIII, 1530.

[12] 27 Henry VIII, c. 25, 1536.

[13] W. J. Ashley, *An Introduction to English Economic History and Theory*, I, part ii, 357.

[14] Nicholls, *op. cit.*, p. 123.

man as an unfortunate brother had been supplemented by the doctrine that the giving of alms was efficacious in saving the soul of the giver. The monasteries had become the centers from which hordes of idle poor were maintained. The suppression of the monasteries, which greatly increased the number of vagabonds and wandering beggars, was followed by the enactment of the most severe laws for the suppression of begging and the punishment of idleness. But while these laws were for the most part but a temporary makeshift, they made one important contribution toward the development of the English Poor Law in their provision for the establishment of almshouses. The local authorities were authorized to provide "tenantries, cottages, and other convenient houses for the lodging of the impotent."[15]

During the reigns of Edward VI and of Elizabeth there was a rapid development of the principle that the poor should be supported by taxation. The method of collecting alms for the support of the poor was revised to provide that persons appointed by the officials of the town and by the church to collect alms should on a particular Sunday "gently ask and demand of every man and woman what they of their charity would give weekly toward the relief of the poor." If any one able to give refused to do so, he was first to be "gently exhorted" by the parson and churchwardens; then, if he still refused, he was to be "persuaded" by the bishop.[16] The system of voluntary contributions probably failed, even with the persuasion of the bishop, to yield adequate

[15] Ashley, *op. cit.*, p. 359.
[16] 5 and 6 Edward VI, c. 2.

funds. At any rate, we find it provided, in 1563, that
if any person after being "gently exhorted" by the parson
and "persuaded" by the bishop, should "obstinately refuse" to contribute to the poor fund, the bishop should
have authority to require a bond of ten pounds for his
appearance "at the next sessions," when the justices, if
the offender remained obstinate, might in their discretion
assess against him the amount which he must pay under
penalty of imprisonment.[17] Finally, in 1572, we reach the
full recognition of the principle that the poor should be
supported by means of a tax levied by the justices of
the peace, the funds to be administered by overseers of
the poor, who themselves were appointed by the justices
of the peace.[18]

Within the latter part of the long period covered by
this brief summary there had developed a special method
of dealing with one class of dependents. In 1535 a law
provided that justices of the peace, constables, and other
local officials should have authority to take up all children between the ages of five and fourteen years who
were begging or in idleness, and apprentice them to be
taught some craft by which they might earn their living
when they should come of age.[19] In 1576 an attempt
was made to provide for the support of illegitimate children, or rather to relieve society of the support of such
children. After stating that bastards "are now left to be
kept at the charge of the parish where they were born,
to the great burthen and defrauding of the relief of the

[17] 5 Elizabeth, c. 3, 1563.
[18] 14 Elizabeth, 1572.
[19] Nicholls, *op. cit.*, p. 124; 27 Henry VIII.

impotent aged true poor of the same parish, and to the evil example and encouragement of lewd life," the act directed the justices of the peace to charge the mother and the reputed father with the support of the child by the payment weekly of such sums of money or other sustenance as the justice should think necessary.[20]

Finally the principles and practices of poor relief which had been slowly developing through six centuries of legislative effort to deal with the problems of pauperism were set forth in the famous 43 Elizabeth which has been termed the "foundation and text-book of the English Poor Law."[21] The poor by this act were divided into three classes: the able-bodied—"rogues," "sturdy vagabonds," and "valiant beggars"; the impotent poor; and children. The able-bodied were to be provided with work in houses of correction. The impotent poor were to be maintained in almshouses. Dependent children were to be apprenticed—boys until they were twenty-four years old and girls until they were twenty-one or were married.[22] In every parish from two to four substantial householders selected by the justices of the peace should serve with the churchwardens as overseers of the poor. These overseers, under the general supervision of the justices of the peace, were to raise by taxation such sums as were necessary for the relief of the poor. The justices of the peace were given authority to commit to the houses of correction or to the common jails any poor person who refused to work as directed by the overseers of the poor.[23]

[20] *Ibid.*, p. 165; 18 Elizabeth, c. 3.

[21] *Ibid.*, p. 189.

[22] Queen, *op. cit.*, p. 186; 43 Elizabeth.

[23] Nicholls, *op. cit.*, p. 191.

Vagrants and beggars were to be returned to the place of their birth or to the place where they had last dwelt for one year.[24]

In 1697 the Bristol workhouse designed to serve a union of the various parishes of that city was authorized by parliament. This was followed by others, and the "workhouse test" inaugurated in 1601 by 43 Elizabeth became an important part of the technique of the administration of poor relief in England. A little later (1723) it was provided that parishes might farm out the poor on contract. Thus was begun the practice of letting the care of the poor to the lowest bidder.[25]

Every act for the relief of the poor contained provisions for the suppression of begging and vagabondage. Some of the earlier laws had as their aim the subjection of the laborer to the landed class. The punishments prescribed for the enforcement of these laws were severe, often brutal. Every poor law enacted prior to 43 Elizabeth, 1601, proclaimed in the preamble that the purpose of the law was to protect society against beggars and vagabonds.[26] 14 Elizabeth, 1573, is typical. This law is entitled "An Act for the Punishment of Vagabonds and for the Relief of the Poor and Impotent." The preamble begins with the statement that "all parts of this realm of England and Wales be presently with rogues, vagabonds, and sturdy beggars exceedingly pestered, by means whereof daily happeneth horrible murders, thefts, and other great outrages, to the high displeasure of Almighty God,

[24] 43 Elizabeth.

[25] Queen, *op. cit.*, p. 190; Nicholls, *op. cit.*, p. 353.

[26] Nicholls, *op. cit.*, p. 189.

and to the great annoyance of the commonwealth."[27]

By the time of the establishment of the colonies in America, then, England had developed a system of poor relief and a code of laws defining the principles of this system which were to remain in effect in that country without fundamental change until the second quarter of the nineteenth century, and in North Carolina until the twentieth. Beginning with the purpose of suppressing begging, of making each community in some measure responsible for its own poor, and of keeping the laborer subservient to the propertied class, the English advanced slowly to the more definite recognition of the claims upon the community of the impotent poor; to the relief of this class through voluntary contributions under the supervision of the church; to the recognition of the fact that the able-bodied poor may not always be able to find work; to the recognition of the dependent child as a peculiar social problem and the attempt to solve that problem by the apprenticeship system; to a consideration of the problem of the illegitimate child, with the emphasis here, it is true, on the protection of the public from the expense of the support of the child; to the definite establishment of the responsibility of each community for the care of its own poor; to the establishment of the principle that the care of the poor is a social problem to be solved by taxation. But the English had never fully divested themselves of the idea that poverty is culpable or at least that society must be protected against the designing poor. Always in the background loomed the workhouse.

[27] *Ibid.*, p. 157.

CHAPTER II

THE COLONIAL PERIOD

SOCIAL conditions in North Carolina in the colonial period were, to quote Captain Ashe, "Arcadian in their simplicity." The inhabitants at the close of the Revolutionary War numbered about 350,000, including slaves, "widely scattered, nearly one-tenth beyond the distant mountains; with no city—and indeed only a few villages whose population reached a thousand; . . . there were no manufactures save the work of men and women in their homes; . . . poor markets and only bad highways; no newspapers and not a single printing press; but few schools, and religious instruction but scantily supplied."[1] "Life offered no field of activity but on the farm and in the forests; and clearing new land and making forest products were the only openings for energy and enterprise."[2] "There were no buggies, but few coaches, and traveling was on horseback, men riding their own horses hundreds of miles, and women seldom visiting out of their neighborhood."[3]

In the earlier days, and largely through the whole period, life in the colony was that of the frontier. The people lived in log houses, covered with hand-riven boards held in place by the weight of poles or fastened by wooden pegs which took the place of nails. "Most of the houses in this part of the country," says Byrd,

[1] S. A. Ashe, *History of North Carolina*, II, 1-2.
[2] *Ibid.*, p. 3.
[3] *Ibid.*, p. 6.

"are log-houses, covered with pine or cypress shingles, three feet long and one broad. They are hung upon laths with peggs, and their doors too turn upon wooden hinges, and have wooden locks to secure them, so that the building is finished without nails or other iron-work."[4]

Writing in 1709, Reverend William Gordon, missionary to the colony, said that the people of Chowan Precinct "indeed are ignorant, there being few that can read, and fewer write, even of their justices of peace and vestrymen." In Perquimans Precinct, he continued, "are twelve vestrymen as in the rest, but most, if not all of them, very ignorant, loose in their lives, and unconcerned as to religion." "Here and in Chowan," he said, "the ways of living are much alike; both are equally destitute of good water, most of that being brackish and muddy; they feed generally upon salt pork, and sometimes upon beef, and their bread of Indian corn which they are forced for want of mills to beat; and in this they are so careless and uncleanly that there is but little difference between the corn in the horse's manger and the bread on their tables; so that with such provisions and such drink (for they have no beer) in such a hot country, you may easily judge, sir, what a comfortable life a man must lead; not but that the place is capable of better things, were it not overrun with sloth and poverty." In Pasquotank Precinct he found the people more industrious, careful, and cleanly. But "in this as in all parts of the province, there is no money; every one buys and pays with their commodities of which corn, pork,

[4] J. S. Bassett, *The Writings of Colonel William Byrd of Westover in Virginia*, p. 78.

pitch, and tar are the chief." Prices for these commodities
fixed by law were so high that one-third of the amount
in English money was preferred.[5] "Among the planters,"
we are told, on the other hand, "were gentry who lived
as much like their relations in England and Scotland
as conditions in a sparsely settled country would admit."[6]
These gentry were highly educated and cultured, entitled
to affix to their wills and other papers "signatures with
seals bearing imprinted thereon crests and coats of
arms,"[7] and able to live in leisure and comparative
luxury, supported by the labor of Negro and Indian
slaves, convicts, and indentured white servants. But this
class, however important in the history of the political
leadership of the colony, evidently formed only a small
part of the whole population. The masses were poor.
That there was, apparently, little suffering beyond the
ordinary hardships of pioneer life, and no great amount
of pauperism, is due to the fact that the mildness of the
climate and the abundance of game made subsistence easy.

But there was want. The lot of the convicts and indentured servants (although these classes were not so
large in North Carolina as in some of the other colonies),[8]
here as elsewhere was especially hard. One catches in the
records occasional glimpses of conditions that must not
have been rare. Indentured servants were allowed, at
the expiration of their terms of service three barrels of
Indian corn and two suits of clothes, and were "entitled

[5] *Colonial Records of North Carolina*, I, 712-15.

[6] J. Bryan Grimes, *Notes on Colonial North Carolina, 1700-
1750*, p. 20.

[7] *Loc. cit.*

[8] Grimes, *op. cit.*, p. 32.

to fifty acres of land which they seldom took up,"[9] partially, it may have been, because of the conditions as to occupancy.[10] That they did not always get the corn and the clothes without difficulty is shown by this entry in the records of the Perquimans Court, March 2, 1703:

Upon a petition of Jeane Richards declaring herself to be a late servant of Mr. Jno. Hacklefield and being now free humbly prays Corne & Cloathes as usuall She taking oath that tis justly due her.
Ordered that Mr. Jno. Hacklefield pay unto Jeane Richards his late Servt. Corne and Cloathes according as the Law in that case provides with Cost also execution.[11]

But Jeane's troubles were not ended. At the preceding meeting of the court on February 9th the following entry had been made:

Samuel Charles as Constable Informs against one Jeane Richards a late Servt. to Mr. Jno. Hacklefield that said Jeane is lately delivered of a bastard child within this precinct and being thereby guilty of the breach of the penall Laws ordered that Sd Jeane be Summon's at ye next Coarte held for the precinct of Perquimans to answer to such things may be aleadged agt. her.[12]

Consequently at the March term we have this entry:

Whereas upon an Information of Samuel Charles against Jeane Richards having a bastard child the said Jeane Richards appearing takes oath that Larence Arnold is the only father to her said child. Ordered that the said

[9] *Loc. cit.*
[10] *Colonial Records of North Carolina,* I, 170.
[11] *Ibid.,* p. 579.
[12] *Ibid.,* p. 576.

Jeane Richards recive twenty one stripes according as the act of Assembly in that case hath provided.[13]

After this double disgrace Jeane's three barrels of corn and two suits of clothes can hardly have opened up an easy financial way for her and her baby, especially as there is no record that the father of the child was made to assume any responsibility for its support.

In 1706 Elizabeth Fitz Garrett, a servant, was convicted of a similar offense and sentenced to serve her master two additional years. At the same time it was ordered that the child should serve the same master until he was twenty-one years old.[14]

In 1727 there appears in the records of the general court at Edenton the case of another indentured servant, Ann Thomas, who after having been sold from one master to another was forced to go to court to obtain the few clothes and the little corn allowed her at the expiration of her term of service.[15] There must have been a considerable number who did not have the courage or the initiative to go to law to enforce their rights.

Among the missionaries sent to the colony of North Carolina by the English Church was one John Urmstone, a man, if one may judge from his letters, of no very high ideals. These letters, however, throw some light on the question of indentured servants in the colony. In 1716, in connection with a request for four Negroes, he observed that "white servants are seldom worth keep-

[13] *Ibid.*, p. 579.
[14] *Ibid.*, p. 655.
[15] *Ibid.*, II, 698.

ing and never stay out their time indentured for."[16] Three years later, again complaining about inadequate funds to supply himself with desirable servants, he writes:

I have only a sorry wretch that I came by on the Ships account and hath but a year and a half to serve, she knows nothing of household affairs and a notorious whore and thief, and yet preferable to any that can be hired here notwithstanding all her faults. She was bred a trader in Spitlefields but followed the Musick Houses most and other vile courses which brought her to Bridewell and from thence transported hither.[17]

Two years later he complains that he has been forced to turn his own son adrift "for his undutifulness in combining with my Servants to ruin me he got a servant wench with child who had two years to serve rendered her not only useless but even a burden to me."[18]

Occasionally there is a glimpse of a more pleasing phase of this picture of the indentured servant. Thomas Pollock in his will made in 1722 leaves forty pounds to Elizabeth Hawkins, wife of Thomas Hawkins of South Shore, Bertie County, who had served him two years after the expiration of her term of servitude.[19]

These convicts and other indentured servants, exploited, despised, and often shiftless, must have formed a considerable group always on the borderland of pauperism. Within the colonial period it was continuously charged from without, but stoutly denied within, that North Carolina was a haven for all undesirable classes, such as

[16] *Ibid.*, p. 261.
[17] *Ibid.*, p. 371.
[18] *Ibid.*, p. 417.
[19] *State Records of North Carolina*, XXII, 296.

pirates, runaway servants and slaves, and criminals. For many years Virginia complained officially cf North Carolina's shortcomings in this respect.[20] In 1699 the attorney-general of Virginia complained that slaves from that colony were harbored after escaping to the south.[21] In reply, Governor Walker protested that neither from her laws nor her practices did North Carolina deserve such a reputation,[22] whereupon the Governor of Virginia declared himself delighted to know that North Carolina had such laws, but suggested that laws which are not vigorously enforced may not "signify much."[23] In 1711 Governor Spottswood in a letter to the Earl of Rochester declared that "North Carolina has long been the common Sanctuary of all our Runaway Servants and of all others that fly from the due execution of the laws."[24] Byrd expressed the opinion that certain mulattoes whom he encountered in running the boundary line, and who passed as free Negroes, were in fact runaway slaves.[25] A letter from Jamaica, dated June 2, 1741, to the Duke of Newcastle in regard to the raising of recruits in the American colonies for the Carthaginian expedition declared that none were "to be expected from Virginia, Maryland, or North Carolina who were not Irish, Papists, or English convicts."[26] North Carolina, at best, seems to have been fortunate in respect to the transportation into

[20] *Colonial Records of North Carolina*, I, 371, 536, 541, 757.
[21] *Ibid.*, p. 513.
[22] *Ibid.*, p. 514.
[23] *Ibid.*, p. 515.
[24] *Ibid.*, p. 798.
[25] Bassett, *op. cit.*, p. 47.
[26] *State Records of North Carolina*, XV, 753.

her borders of convicts and other undesirables only in that not having one of the principal ports of entry, she did not receive so many as some of the other colonies. The numbers from these classes which she received directly were doubtlessly increased by others who had been transported to the adjoining colonies. And settlers from these classes, voluntary and involuntary, were necessarily poor, many of them on the verge of dependency.

Among other classes of colonists there must also have been much poverty bordering on penury. There were early marriages and consequently large families. Lawson observed that the women married very young, some at thirteen and fourteen, and that at twenty a young woman was considered a stale maid.[27] Governor Arthur Dobbs, in 1755, wrote: "There are at present 75 families on my lands. I viewed betwixt 30 and 40 of them and except two there was not less than from 5 to 6 to 10 children in each family, each going barefooted in their shifts in warm weather no woman wearing more than a shift and one thin petticoat."[28]

It was therefore upon a society of frontiersmen, with a considerable group of involuntary immigrants from the derelicts of English society, that the principles and practices of poor relief of England at that period, already transplanted to the colony of Virginia, were imposed by statute a hundred years after the first adventurers had wandered into the forests of North Carolina from the colony to the north.

The earliest record of poor relief legislation in North

[27] John Lawson, *History of North Carolina*, p. 47.
[28] *Colonial Records of North Carolina*, V, 555.

Carolina is of the introduction in the colonial assembly
on Friday, April 7, 1749, of a bill for the relief of the
poor and the prevention of idleness.[29] This bill was before the assembly again on the eighth[30] and the eleventh
of April.[31] The same matter came up a third time in
the lower house on the seventh[32] and again on the ninth
of October of the same year,[33] and on the eleventh was
passed by this branch of the assembly and sent to the
council.[34] On the twelfth the house was notified of the
rejection of the bill by the council.[35]

On the second of October, 1755, a bill for the restraint
of vagrants and for making provision for the poor was
introduced in the colonial assembly. The record reads:
"Indorst in the Assembly, read the first time and passed.
In the upper house read the first time and passed."[36] This
bill became a law on the fifteenth of October, 1755.[37] It
is entitled, "An Act for the Restraint of Vagrants, and
for Making Provision for the Poor, and for Other Purposes." It contains the following provisions:

1. All persons are forbidden to entertain, hire, or employ for more than forty-eight hours any person being
taxable and removing from another parish unless such
person has a certificate from the sheriff or a magistrate

[29] *Colonial Records of North Carolina*, IV, 977.
[30] *Ibid.*, pp. 978, 992, 993.
[31] *Ibid.*, p. 980.
[32] *Ibid.*, p. 1003.
[33] *Ibid.*, p. 1013.
[34] *Ibid.*, p. 1016.
[35] *Ibid.*, p. 1017.
[36] *Ibid.*, V, 502.
[37] *Ibid.*, p. 558.

of the county from which he came showing that he had paid his taxes or was not taxable.

2. A vagabond must furnish security, be bound to service, or if no one will take him or her, be whipped—thirty-nine lashes on his or her bare back.

3. "That upon complaint made by the Church Wardens of any Parish before a Justice of the Peace, that any Person or Persons is or are come into their Parish, and likely to become chargeable thereto, it shall be lawful for such Justice by Warrant, under his Hand, to cause such poor Person to be removed to the Parish where he or she was legally last settled; but if such poor person be sick or disabled and cannot be removed without Danger of Life, the Church Wardens shall provide for his or her maintenance and Cure, at the Charge of the Parish and after recovery shall cause him or her to be so removed; and the Parish wherein he or she was last legally settled shall repay all charges. . . . And if the Church Wardens or Wardens of the Parish to which such poor person belongs shall refuse to receive and provide for the Person or Persons removed by warrant aforesaid, every Church Warden so refusing shall forfeit and pay Twenty Pounds, Proclamation Money; one-half to our Sovereign Lord the King for the use of the Parish from whence the Removal was and the other Moity to the Informer."[38]

Four years later we have another act prefaced as follows: "Whereas, it is absolutely necessary that a Vestry be Immediately appointed for each parish within the

[38] *State Records of North Carolina*, XXIII, 436.

Province to make provision for the Clergy and support of the Poor," and providing that persons then vestrymen should be legally appointed vestrymen in their respective parishes; that parishes not having acting vestrymen should elect such officials by a vote of the freeholders; and that a poll tax should be levied for the paying of the salary of the minister, the support of the poor, and other parish expenses.[39]

In 1760 the assembly again enacted a law to make provision for the pay of the clergy and the support of the poor. Under this act the freeholders of each parish were to elect twelve vestrymen. Any freeholder failing to vote was liable to a fine of twenty shillings. The vestry thus elected were to select two churchwardens who were to have active charge of the relief of the poor.[40]

The freeholders of the colony, however, do not seem to have been greatly impressed either by their duty to the poor or by the threat of a fine of twenty shillings for not voting. One strongly suspects that the political leaders of the day were simply following the precedent of the mother country and were attempting to adopt the conventional laws of England in regard to the support of the church, the suppression of idleness, and the relief of the poor. The masses were apparently indifferent to any sort of church and certainly had no enthusiasm for an established church; they seem to have had no particular prejudice against idleness; and they probably did not yet see the need for public poor relief. At any rate, the next year we have an additional act for the election

[39] *State Records of North Carolina*, XXV, 396.
[40] *Ibid.*, p. 424.

of vestries in parishes that "have no legal vestries to make provision for the poor," etc.[41]

Three years later, in 1764, we again have an act beginning: "Whereas making provision for the Clergy, providing for the Poor, and the due management of Parochial Affairs require that a Vestry be established in each Parish in this Province," and providing for the election by the freeholders of each parish of twelve freeholders to serve as vestrymen; for the election by the vestrymen of two churchwardens; and for the levy by the vestry of a poll tax not to exceed ten shillings "for building Churches and Chappels, paying the Minister's Salary, purchasing a Glebe, erecting a Mansion and convenient Outhouses thereon, encouraging Schools, maintaining the poor, paying clerks and readers, and defraying other incidental Charges of the Parish."[42]

In 1766 the act of 1755 was continued for four years[43] and again in 1770 for five years.[44]

In 1771 it was enacted that "Whereas the Poor of the Parish of St. John in the County of Pasquotank labour under great Distress by Reason that Persons heretofore elected to constitute a Vestry have neglected to qualify and Act agreeable to Law," the freeholders of the parish were empowered to elect vestrymen.[45]

This is the record of the legislation in the colony of North Carolina. There is nothing new here, nothing in advance of the ideals and practices of England. The

[41] *Ibid.*, p. 450.
[42] *Ibid.*, XXIII, 601.
[43] *Ibid.*, p. 678.
[44] *Ibid.*, p. 831.
[45] *Ibid.*, p. 853.

colony, in so far as ideals and methods of poor relief as expressed in her laws are concerned, was thoroughly loyal to the mother country. There was very little change to adapt these ideals and methods to the new country. As to the administration of the laws the colonists left little record. The method of providing for dependent children by apprenticing them in vogue in England at the period was practised in North Carolina from the earliest days and continued until the enactment of the juvenile court law in 1919. There is record of such apprenticeship as early as 1695,[46] and the practice, as evidenced by the records, was in common use thereafter. This matter is treated at some length in Chapter VII. Of the administration of what is ordinarily included under the term *poor relief* but little record has been preserved. Most officers charged with the immediate care of the poor have apparently at no period in the history of North Carolina considered it important to preserve records of their transactions. For the colonial period we have the vestry book of the Parish of Saint Pauls, Chowan Precinct, from 1701 to 1715. In this parish at least there appears not to have been any great amount of poverty that in the opinion of the vestrymen demanded relief from public funds. There are enough instances of relief in the record, however, to give a fair idea of the practices of the period. Under the date of April 4, 1703, there appears this entry:

Whereas Robert Wilson who was kept by William Brethel for the space of two or three months upon Precinct Charge and is dead and Coll. Wilkinson declaring

[46] *Colonial Records of North Carolina*, I, 448.

that he has paid unto the said Brethell for the care and keeping of said Willson the Sum of eight pounds, which was the full Consideration for one whole year.

Ordered that William Brethell shall reimburse Coll. William Wilkinson the aforesaid Eight pounds except So much as he shall make appear to have disburst for his Burial and the time he kept Him—[47]

From the same record and for the same date we read:

Information being made by Capt. Thomas Blount that Elenor Adams by of Infirmity and Indigence is in great Danger of being lost for want of assistance.

The Same being taken into Consideration—

Ordered that Captt. Thomas Blount treat with Doct. Godfrey Spruill in order to her Cure and that Doctor Godfrey Spruill be paid for his physick and Care by the Church Wardens five pounds and Capt. Thomas Blount is requested by Vestry to endeavor to oblige the Said Elenor to Serve the Doctor for the use of his House and nursing.[48]

At the end of the year this item appears in the list of bills paid.[49] There is no record as to what service, if any, Elenor rendered to the doctor for the use of his house and for nursing.

On May 26, 1704, this entry was made:

Ordered that three pounds be paid Richard Booth toward the maintenance of an orphan child left destitute by Stephen Preston.[50]

The same order was made again on January 3, 1706,[51] and on April 18, 1708, we note the following:

[47] *Ibid.*, p. 569.
[48] *Loc. cit.*
[49] *Colonial Records of North Carolina*, I, 577.
[50] *Ibid.*, p. 600.
[51] *Ibid.*, p. 630.

Richard Booth having had an allowance of three pounds per annum for maintaining an orphan child of Stephen Besson's comes here and assumes to keep and maintain the child without further charge.

Apparently this arrangement was accepted without imposing any definite obligations on Booth.[52]

On April 18, 1708:

On petition of Madam Mary Blount for accommodating a poor, indigent man named Thomas Wright at her house, in his sickness one week, whereof he died and was buried at her charge, prays allowance.

Ordered that she be paid by the public forty shillings.[53]

These meager records indicate, as has already been said, that there was no great demand upon the public purse for the relief of the poor. To any one familiar with recent methods of administering poor relief by boards of county commissioners these excerpts from the records of an earlier day will have a familiar look. From 1700 to 1900 there was practically no change in the method of administering the poor funds. In colonial days some citizen appeared before the vestrymen and stated that a certain poor person needed aid or stated that he himself had relieved such a poor person and asked to be reimbursed from the public funds. Upon such representation relief was given. This is just the method that until 1919 was followed by the county commissioners in all the counties of the state and that is still in use in several of the counties.[54] In colonial times and in all subsequent periods, down at least to 1919,

[52] *Ibid.*, p. 678.
[53] *Ibid.*, p. 679.
[54] See pp. 133 ff.

children who were public charges were liable to be handed over, without any specific guarantee as to their treatment, to any one who was willing to relieve the public of the expense of their maintenance. The grants of the colonial vestries in 1700 for relief seem to have been quite as liberal as the grants of county commissioners in 1900. On the other hand, compared with the past rather than with the future, in methods of administration as well as in legislation, the colonists appear to have been following as nearly as possible the tradition and practices of England.

CHAPTER III

UNDER THE WARDENS OF THE POOR, 1776-1868

THE Revolution brought no important change in the theory or practice of poor relief in North Carolina. The principles and methods developed in England and transplanted to the colony continued to be the principles and methods of the new state. In 1777 the law was revised to conform to the new order inaugurated by the Revolution. The new law provided that the freemen of every county elect seven freeholders as overseers of the poor. These overseers were to hold their positions for three years. They in turn were to elect two of their number wardens of the poor. The overseers of the poor succeeded to all the powers, duties, and obligations of the former vestries of the parishes. They were empowered to levy a tax not to exceed six pence on every one hundred pounds value of taxable property and a poll tax of six pence on all persons not having an estate of one hundred pounds. The law as to removal of poor persons to the place of legal settlement was changed to read "county" for "parish" and "county" for "king"; that is, the county rather than the parish became the unit of administration, and forfeitures were made to the county instead of to the King. Legal settlement was acquired by one year's residence in the county.[1]

In 1799 the tax rate for the support of the poor was increased to one shilling six pence on the hundred

[1] *State Records of North Carolina*, XXIV, 89.

2. THE LAST OF ITS KIND

This is one of several log cabins that make up the county home in Yadkin County

pounds.[2] The next year this tax was declared by legislative enactment to be inadequate by far and a poor rate of five shillings was authorized.[3]

That opposition or indifference to the support of the poor did not cease with the disestablishment of the church and the transfer of sovereignty from the king to the people is indicated by an act of 1781 which declared that many overseers of the poor refused or neglected to qualify and that the poor were "reduced to great distress to the scandal and disgrace of society." This act fixed a penalty of ten pounds for failure to qualify as an overseer of the poor.[4] In 1783 the legislature declared that there were no overseers in many counties and directed the sheriffs of the several delinquent counties to summon the voters to elect such overseers. The poor rate was fixed by this act at one shilling on the one hundred pounds and one shilling on the poll.[5] Two years later, in 1785, an act of the legislature declared that there were still many counties without overseers of the poor and that the sheriffs had neglected to hold elections. Sheriffs were directed to call elections within two months for the election of officials here called wardens of the poor.[6] On December 10, 1816, there was presented in the senate a petition from the wardens of the poor of Craven County asking that the fine for declining to serve as a warden

[2] *Ibid.*, p. 260.
[3] *Ibid.*, p. 318.
[4] *Ibid.*, p. 409.
[5] *Ibid.*, p. 498.
[6] *Ibid.*, p. 783.

be increased for that county from twenty-five dollars to one hundred dollars.[7]

In the same year, 1785, a new step was taken in the legal provision of this state for the care of the poor. The legislature enacted a law by which wardens of the poor in Northampton, Nash, Halifax, Chowan, Carteret, Wayne, and Onslow counties were empowered to purchase land and erect almshouses thereon. The act further provided: "That persons being either distracted or otherwise deprived of their senses, so that the wardens shall judge them incapable of self-preservation, shall be under the care of said wardens, who are empowered to keep them confined in such houses so long as they may judge necessary. A poor tax of two shillings on every poll, eight pence on every one hundred acres of land, and two shillings on every one hundred pounds value in town lots was authorized.[8]

Within the next few years numerous laws regarding the relief of the poor were enacted. In 1786 the act to empower wardens of the poor to build houses for the care of the poor in their counties was extended to include Chatham County.[9]

In 1787 the tax for the relief of the poor was fixed by the Assembly at a rate not to exceed two shillings on the poll and eight pence on an acre of land. At the same time it was declared that several counties were without wardens. It was provided that the sheriffs of the several counties, at any time that it might be necessary, should

[7] Legislative MS.
[8] State Records of North Carolina, XXIV, 739.
[9] Ibid., p. 884.

summon the people to elect seven "good and sufficient freeholders" to be wardens of the poor.[10] By another act of 1787 the counties of Warren, Caswell, Pasquotank, Halifax, Johnston, Richmond, Hyde, Martin, Wake, Rockingham, and Hertford were authorized to build houses for the poor: "Provided, that this act shall not be construed so as to oblige the wardens to lay any tax for any of the said counties unless they find the same necessary."[11]

The legislature of 1789 empowered the counties of Franklin, Surry, and Orange to build houses for the care of the poor. In the case of Surry it was provided "that persons being incapable to support themselves or of self-preservation, shall be under the care of said wardens, who are empowered to dispose of them in said houses"; and that such of the inmates of the almshouse as were able to work should be "employed on some suitable business for the benefit of such poor."[12]

An act of 1790 again empowered the counties of Pasquotank and Carteret to build houses for the care of the poor and named a commission of three in each county to have charge of the matter. These commissioners were authorized to purchase two acres of land in each county and to erect houses thereon for the reception of the poor. The wardens were authorized to admit to these houses such persons of both sexes as they should judge incapable by reason of old age or infirmity of procuring sustenance for themselves. The wardens were also empowered to ap-

[10] *Ibid.*, p. 940.
[11] *Ibid.*, p. 947.
[12] *Ibid.*, XXV, 60.

point a keeper or overseer of the poorhouse whose duty it should be to preserve good order among the poor and to enforce the regulations established by the wardens. Inmates who were able to work should "be moderately employed and kept at such labor and the profits thereof applied to the support of the poor of the county."[13]

One of the most interesting bits of legislation of this period is an act of 1787 relating to the care of the poor in Craven County. This act indicates that while our ideas as to the proper methods of raising money for public purposes have changed somewhat, complaints as to the variety and burden of taxes are not peculiar to our own day. The law reads in part as follows:

Whereas, it would tend very much to the relief of the inhabitants of the county of Craven to have a house built for the reception of the poor in said county; and whereas it would be difficult, from the variety of taxes now levied on said inhabitants, to raise a sufficient sum by a tax, and it is thought that a sum adequate to the purpose aforesaid may be raised by lottery: Be it enacted by the General Assembly of the State of North Carolina and it is hereby enacted by the authority of the same, That Richard Dobbs Spaight, John Wright Stanley, John Hawkins, Spyers Singleton, and Abner Neal, Esquires, shall be and they are hereby appointed managers, who, or a majority, of them, shall undertake, carry on, and draw a lottery in New Bern, for the purposes aforesaid, with power to issue two thousand tickets for the first class at twenty shillings each, and two thousand tickets for the second class at thirty shillings each, the tickets to be signed by themselves and to be in the following Form: "No.____ Craven County poorhouse lottery. This ticket entitles the bearer to whatever prize may be drawn

[13] *Ibid.*, p. 68.

against this number, deducting fifteen per cent, as per act of Assembly passed in December, 1786."

The act further provided for the details of conducting the lottery. The money realized from the lottery was to be turned over to the wardens of the poor of the county who were directed to purchase three acres of land and erect the poorhouse.[14]

But the poorhouse in Craven was not built under this plan. In 1817[15] there was an act empowering the local authorities to build a poorhouse by the ordinary prosaic method of levying a tax. In 1808 Brunswick County was authorized to raise money for a poorhouse by one or more lotteries.[16] She seems to have been no more successful than Craven; for a later local act authorized the establishment of a poorhouse and the raising of the money for this purpose by a tax.

In 1793, by a state-wide law, the wardens of the poor were empowered to build houses for the care of the poor in their respective counties. "And the said wardens are likewise empowered, when to them or at least two-thirds of them in each county it appears necessary, to erect proper buildings in their respective counties for the reception, residence and employment of the poor."[17]

The public laws of 1817, chapter 13, provided that a tax sufficient for the relief of the poor should be levied, upon application of the wardens of the poor, by the

[14] *Ibid.*, XXIV, 821.

[15] *Public Laws of North Carolina, 1817*, chap. 84.

[16] *Public Laws of North Carolina, 1808*, chap. 118.

[17] *Public Acts of the General Assembly of North Carolina*, vol. II (1790-1803). Compiled by F. X. Martin.

court of pleas and quarter sessions presided over by the
justices of the peace of the county.

From 1793 to 1830 there were enacted numerous laws
authorizing specific counties to establish houses for the
care of the poor, called in many of these laws "poor and
workhouses."[18] Some of these acts enumerated the classes
of offenders who might be sent by the courts to these
institutions.[19] They included vagrants, gamblers,
and prostitutes. The usual procedure proposed by
these acts for building such poorhouses was that the
wardens of the poor should make application to the
justices of the county court of pleas and quarter sessions
for the levy of a tax for the purpose.[20] Sometimes the
wardens were authorized to proceed directly on their
own authority.[21] Sometimes the justices of the county
court were empowered to act.[22] Occasionally a special
commission was provided for.[23] There was, however,
considerably more interest in the subject among the law-
makers than among the people of the various counties
or their local officials. For many years the passage of
an act of the legislature authorizing the building of a
poorhouse did not carry even the probability that it
would be built. For Pasquotank County, for example,
no less than half a dozen local acts as well as two state-
wide acts authorizing the building of such an institution
had been passed by the legislature before a poorhouse

[18] *Public Laws of North Carolina, 1824*, chap. 62.
[19] *Public Laws of North Carolina, 1817*, chap. 84.
[20] *Public Laws of North Carolina, 1824*, chap. 62.
[21] *Public Laws of North Carolina, 1817*, chap. 84.
[22] *Public Laws of North Carolina, 1824*, chap. 63.
[23] *Public Laws of North Carolina, 1825*, chap. 121.

was opened in that county.   Several other counties have a similar history.

It was during this long period of approximately half a century of legislative agitation concerning poor relief, apparently, that the idea of the possibility of farming operations on a considerable scale in connection with the almshouse took shape.   Some of the earlier acts specify two or three acres[24] as a desirable amount of land to be procured for the poorhouse.   Some of the later acts of the period, on the other hand, suggest two or three hundred acres[25] as the desirable amount.   It is significant, also, that whereas in the earlier acts the institutions are referred to as houses for the care of the poor, in several of the later acts they are called poor- and work-houses.   The idea had developed that the poor might be supported wholly or mainly by their own labor or by their labor supplemented by that of certain classes of misdemeanants.

In 1831 we have again a state-wide act providing for the erection of poorhouses in the various counties.   This act reads:

The court of pleas and quarter sessions of the several counties shall be and they are hereby authorized, when they deem it necessary, a majority of the justices of said court being present, to cause to be erected poor houses and other buildings for the maintenance and support of the poor of said counties, with full power and authority to purchase lands when the same may be necessary.

The act further provides:

[24] *State Records of North Carolina*, XXIV, 822.
[25] *Public Laws of North Carolina, 1825*, chap. 136.

The wardens of the poor of said counties, twenty days
notice at least being given, shall annually let out to the
lowest bidder the said poor houses and the poor of their
respective counties, or shall employ some person as
overseer to superintend the business, as to them may seem
best, such contractor or overseer giving bond and approved security for the faithful discharge of the duties
assigned to him; and the wardens shall have full power
and authority to ordain by-laws, rules and regulations;
and do all such matters and things as they may deem
expedient, for the promotion of the said poor house, and
the comfort of the poor.[26]

For several years there had been some interest in
such a general law. On December 22, 1825, a committee of the senate had reported that while

the laws concerning pauperism and parishioners might
by a revisal, be much amended, that at present so many
counties have private laws on the subject, that it would
be difficult to establish any general plans.[27]

And again on January 2, 1827, the Committee on Judi-
ciary in the senate having under consideration the
proposition of a general law for the erection of poor-
and workhouses, reported:

That inasmuch as many counties have already erected
such houses and as a diversity of opinion prevails in
different counties, and in some instances in the same
county, regarding the advantages and policy of such es-
tablishments, your committee deem it inexpedient to pass
a general law on the subject.[28]

The revised code of 1854, codifying the laws to that

[26] *Revised Statutes of North Carolina, 1837,* p. 474.
[27] Legislative MS.
[28] Legislative MS.

date, provided (chapter 86) that the justices of the several courts of pleas and quarter sessions should elect every three years not more than twelve nor fewer than seven freeholders to serve as wardens of the poor in their respective counties. The wardens thus elected— styled when organized "the court of wardens"—were directed to elect one of their number treasurer and some fit person, not of their number, clerk. Any three wardens might call a court by written summons directed to the sheriff of the county or to any constable. On application of the wardens the justices were empowered to levy a tax sufficient for the support of the poor. The courts of pleas and quarter sessions were further empowered when they deemed it necessary to purchase lands and cause to be erected houses for the maintenance of the poor. The act provided also that "the wardens shall annually let to the lowest bidder, or employ some person as overseer of, the said poor house and poor of their respective counties, as to them may seem best."

By 1854 the law of legal settlement that was to obtain in the state had been fully developed. The law of 1755 provided for the removal of any poor person, liable to become a public charge, to the place of his settlement. The act of 1777 made no material change in this law. The county was made the unit instead of the parish. One year's residence in the county was declared necessary to establish legal settlement. The code of 1854 more precisely defines this term. The married woman has the legal settlement of her husband; the legitimate child, that of its father; the illegitimate child, that of its mother. Settlement is retained until a new one is established.

In addition to the revenues derived from the taxes
authorized from time to time, funds from special sources
were sometimes turned into the poor fund. An act of
the year 1779 reads as follows:

All horses, cattle, hogs, and sheep, that shall belong
to any slave, or be of any slave's mark in this State, shall
be seized and sold by the county wardens, and by them
applied, the one half to the support of the poor of the
county, and the other half to the informer.[29]

In 1839 it was enacted:

That it shall not be lawful for any person or persons,
resident in the State of Virginia to drive any hogs,
horses or cattle into the County of Currituck, for the
purpose of ranging or pasturing on any of the marsh
or pasture lands of said county, and every person or
persons violating the provisions of this Act, shall forfeit
and pay the sum of five dollars for every head of hogs,
horses or cattle, that may be so ranged or pastured, over
ten head for every hundred acres of land he or they may
own in said County, to be recovered before any Justice
of the Peace in the County of Currituck, one half to the
use of the person prosecuting, and the other to the
wardens of the poor.[30]

The most interesting piece of legislation in this connection is perhaps the following:

That if any person shall be intoxicated at a church,
meeting-house, or any other place appointed for divine
worship, in the time people shall be there assembled for
the purpose of divine worship; or shall at such time and
place, quarrel, fight, or be guilty of any other disorder-
ly behavior, he shall forfeit and pay to the use of the poor

[29] *State Records of North Carolina*, XXXV, 260.
[30] *Public Laws of North Carolina, 1838-9*, chap. 52.

of the county in which the offense shall have been committed the sum of two pounds ten shillings.

That an act passed at the last session of the General Assembly entiled, "An act to prevent the selling of spirituous liquors and other articles at church or meeting-house yards on days of divine worship" be, and the same is hereby repealed.[31]

For the period from the Revolution to the Civil War there are but meager records of the administration of poor relief. In the archives of the North Carolina State Historical Commission are preserved the minutes of St. Gabriel's Parish, Duplin County, for the years 1800 to 1817. There are also in the commission's collection the minutes of the wardens of the poor for Pasquotank County for the years 1807 to 1831, the minutes of the wardens of Ashe County from 1832 to 1855, and a few scattering sheets from the records for Franklin County. The library of the Department of Rural Social-Economics of the University of North Carolina has the minute book of the wardens of the poor of Orange County for the period from 1832 to 1856.

From the minutes of St. Gabriel's Parish it appears that there were two methods of relief in use. According to one the wardens made such allowance toward the support of the poor person as in their judgment was necessary.   The following excerpt from the records is typical:

January 1, 1800 County Wardens to Isaac Thomas, to one month's maintenance to Creasy Richman two pounds.

In 1803 Ann Freeman was granted an allowance of

[31] *Public Laws of North Carolina, 1807*, chap. 20.

seven pounds for maintaining her children from January
court to the following April. At the same time it was
ordered that Andrew Rouse, a parishioner, "be allowed
to contract with any person who will find him with sufficient victuals, washing and lodging until the second
day of July court next and that the clerk furnish him
with an attested copy of this order." If it should be considered necessary to furnish him with a few clothes the
wardens agreed to bear that expense also.

The second method of relief in use in Duplin County
in these early days of the period under consideration was
the selling of the maintenance of the pauper to the lowest
bidder. Dated January 1, 1800, this entry appears:

John Screws and child being set up to the lowest bidder was bid off by Stephen Martindale for six months
at twenty-nine pounds. Order that Martindale furnish
said Screws and child with everything necessary for a
person in their situation.

On April twenty-second of the same year:

William Hubbard's child, an illegitimate, was this day
presented to the board of wardens as an object of charity
and received as such, was set up to the lowest bidder,
was bid off by William Albert for three months for four
pounds.

At the same meeting of the wardens it appears that

Stephen Brown, a parishoner, was bid off by Jesse
Brown at fifty pounds for one year.

In 1803 James Jones, whose name appears several
times in the records, was bid off by Lewis Barfield at
the sum of six pounds. It was stipulated that Jones was

to be furnished with "three shirts, three pairs of trousers (one of the latter of yarn), coat and under jacket, a pair of yarn stockings and a pair of shoes."

For the first half of the period covered by the record for Pasquotank County the method in use there was to make grants of a certain sum for a specified period toward the maintenance of the pauper named. These grants were sometimes continued over a number of years. Such a case was that of Hepsebeth Cook who was given aid in the support of her son. The first allowance was granted in October, 1808, and was for forty shillings. This was repeated quarterly until July, 1810. In January, 1811, she was given eighteen pounds for six months, presumably the preceding six months. In April of the same year the grant was eighteen dollars for three months. The next quarter the amount was reduced to fifteen dollars, but was raised to eighteen dollars the following quarter and remained at that figure until October, 1816, when it was raised to twenty-one dollars a quarter. In January, 1817, the allowance was again raised, this time to twenty-four dollars; but it remained at this figure for only one quarter, after which it was reduced to eighteen dollars, remaining at this figure until October, 1820, when it was once more raised to twenty-four dollars, where it remained until April, 1822, the date of the last allowance recorded.

In 1821 the method of administering relief was changed. On April 21 of that year the following entry was made on the minutes of the wardens:

Ordered that the paupers belonging to the County of

Pasquotank be set up to the lowest bidder on Monday the 25th April, 1821.

The record is completed by the following entry:

Elizabeth City, April 25, 1821. Agreeable to an order passed last meeting of the wardens of the poor they proceeded to set up the paupers to the lowest bidder and they were struck off to the following persons: . . .

Here follow the names of the poor and the names of the persons bidding them off. There were twenty-seven persons thus disposed of. Thirteen of these were children. The maintenance of twelve of the children was let to their own mothers. The mother of the other child was herself a county charge. At least two of the adults were probably bid off by relatives. The prices at which the bidders undertook the care of the paupers varied from ninety-five cents to three dollars and fifty cents per month.

While nothing appears in the record at this time to indicate that any exceptions were made in the sale of the paupers to the lowest bidder, that not all of them were so disposed of is shown by the continued quarterly grants for one year to Hepsebeth Cook for the support of her son, whose name does not appear among those let to the lowest bidder.

This system continued for ten years, until 1831, when the newly-built poorhouse was opened. The last list of paupers aided by the county prior to the opening of the poorhouse contained forty-four names besides "Suckey Arnold and children." Toward the maintenance of these poor people the county was paying amounts varying from two dollars and a half to eight dollars per month.

On October 13, 1831, the wardens of the poor ordered that twenty-one persons named in the order be admitted to the county poorhouse. This number included seven children and two Negroes—one, a "negro man Pompey" and "Betsey Sexton's child colored."

The extent of poor relief in Pasquotank is shown for certain years by the total amounts spent for this purpose. From April, 1808, to January, 1809, the total amounted to two hundred ninety-five pounds, eight shillings; for the year 1809, to three hundred twenty-five pounds, two shillings, seven pence; and for 1810, to four hundred forty-four pounds, nine shillings, eight pence. In 1830 the total poor fund amounted to $2,288.12½, and the total expenditures to $3,142.81½. Within this year, however, the poorhouse was built. The following table from the records throws additional light on expenditures for the poor at this period:

Suppose old debt, April, 1829 to be	$2,000.00	Tax is 1828,	$2,176.35
Amount of allowances		1829,	2,084.18
for parochial year		1830,	2,900.00
1829	1,699.49½	Estimated debt	
1830	2,288.12½	Jan. 1832	
1831	1,836.86¼		663.95¼
	$7,824.48¼		$7,824.48¼

The Ashe County record beginning immediately after the close of that for Pasquotank shows no improvement in method. On September 17, 1832, the wardens "contracted with Stephen Mullis to keep Susannah Sparks

twelve months at $100, or," thinking perhaps that
Susannah might die, "in proportion to the time he keeps
her." But Susannah did not die, nor did Mullis keep her
a year, for in May of the next year the wardens "sold
out Susannah Sparks a pauper to Solomon Fonts for six
months at $39," the "selling out" method thus having ap-
parently a considerable advantage from the economic
point of view over the "contract" method. Six months
later they "allowed to Leonard Fonts forty dollars for
keeping Susannah Sparks six months." On May 19, 1834,
"The Wardens for the poor of the County of Ashe met
to wit, William Weaver, Mathew Carson, John Millar,
Jasper Testerman, John Shearer, and James Smith and
made an allowance to Richard Phillips of $24 to keep
Susannah Sparks Six Months."

Since two of the four volumes of wardens' records
discovered begin with the year 1832, it seems probable
that a greater interest in the care of the poor dates from
the enactment of the law of 1831. At any rate the board
of wardens for Orange County which came into office in
the spring of 1832, set about their work in an orderly
and apparently a businesslike way. The record in beautiful script opens with the induction into office of the new
board of wardens:

At a meeting of the Wardens of the Poor for Orange
County at the store of William F. Strudwick and Co. on
the 29th May 1832 in Hillsborough, Thomas D. Watts
returned a certificate that James Webb, James Mebane,
Cadwallader Jones, J. U. Kirkland, Jon P. Sneed, James
Faucette, and James Forrest were duly elected Wardens
of the Poor of Orange County for three years from Easter

3. ORANGE COUNTY HOME

This building, one of two just alike which constitute the living quarters of the Orange County home, has been in use a hundred years

Monday last when the Wardens subscribed and took the following oath:

We the undersigned do swear that we will honestly and faithfully discharge our office of Wardens of the Poor to the best of our skill and ability according to Law.

Sworn and subscribed before me this the 29th May 1832.   HERBERT SIMS, J. P.

To this is attached the names of the wardens. Then follows the certificate of election:

STATE OF NORTH CAROLINA
ORANGE COUNTY

I, Thomas D. Watts, Sheriff of Orange County, do certify that at an election began and held at the Court House in the town of Hillsborough on the 23rd April 1832 for the purpose of electing Wardens of the Poor to serve for the term of three years from this date, that the following persons were duly elected,

> James Mebane Esq.
> Col. Cadwallader Jones
> James Forest Esq.
> James Faucette
> Doctor James Webb
> John U. Kirkland
> Jon P. Sneed, Esq.

THOMAS D. WATTS, *Shff.*
BY
GEORGE LAWS, *D. Shff.*

The first meeting at which routine business of the wardens of the county was transacted, it seems, was in June. The record reads:

POOR HOUSE
9th June 1832.

This day the Wardens of the Poor met according to appointment—Colo. Cad. Jones in the chair and all the members of the board present.

The Court of Wardens upon examination of the premises find them in good order and the situation of the paupers comfortable.

It appearing to the Ct. of Wardens that the last semi-annual account has not been settled it is therefore

Ordered that Mr. Sneed the present Treasr. Mr. Kirkland and the Secretary be and are hereby appointed a committee to settle with the late Treasr. Mr. Josiah Turner and the overseer Mr. Gattis and report to the next meeting of the Ct. of Wardens.

Ordered that the Treasurer purchase a bound book in which it shall be the duty of the Secretary to record the proceedings of the Ct. of Wardens and to keep his accounts.

Ordered that it shall be the duty of the Overseer of the Poor to take an inventory of the effects and property of the county under the care of the Court of Wardens and return it on the 1st October in each and every year.

On motion of Mr. Kirkland ordered that the court of Wardens be divided into committees consisting of two, whose duty it shall be to visit the Poor House on the first Monday of every month to examine into the conditions of the House and the situation of the paupers.

James Forest J. P. Sneed	1st committee
Cad. Jones E. Strudwick	2nd committee
James Mebane James Webb	3rd committee
John U. Kirkland James Faucette	4th committee

The first committee to commence its visits on the first Monday in July next.

Ordered that one or more of the Court of Wardens may give a ticket of admission into the Poor House to any person he or they may think entitled to the charity of the County during the interval of the session of the Court of Wardens and that the overseer receive such person or persons accordingly.

Ordered that the Secretary give public notice in the *Hillsborough Recorder*, that the semi-annual meeting of the Court of Wardens will be held on the first [Monday] in October and April at which time paupers should make application for admission into the Poor House and on the first Monday of October proposals will be received for making a contract with an overseer.

Ordered that Mr. Robert Burnsides account for boarding and nursing Almon Nelson 10 weeks, which was presented by Dr. Webb for payment, be rejected.

Sally Chandler

It appearing to the Court of Wardens that Sally Chandler a crippled pauper may probably be restored to the use of her limbs by a surgical operation, it is ordered that she be taken to Hillsboro and the operation performed.

Ordered that when this Court of Wardens adjourn it adjourn to meet on the first Monday in October next. Whereupon the Court of Wardens adjourned.

By   CAD. JONES, *Chairman.*
    ED STRUDWICK,
        Sect.

At the October meeting the overseer of the poorhouse presented an inventory of "the effects of the County in his possession at the Poor House" and it was "registered" as follows: 1 mule, 1 cart, 2 work oxen, 2 old oxen fattening, 4 cows, 2 yearlings, 9 hogs for the pen, 3 sows, 23 shoats and pigs, 3 ploughs, 2 set plough gear, 2 weeding hoes, 1 mattock, 2 axes, 1 iron wedge, 3 iron pots, 2 ovens, 2 cotton wheels, 2 dozen chairs, 1 grind stone, blankets, beds, sheets, counterpains, 1 scythe, 1 grass scythe, 2 augers, 1 drawing knife, 2 chisels, 1 spade, 1 shovel, 1 dung fork, 1 log chain.

On October 1, 1832, there were twenty-one paupers in the poorhouse. Such an annual census is given for sixteen of the twenty-five years covered by the record. The smallest number on any census day is nineteen in 1835 and 1836. The largest number is forty in 1847. Per capita costs, given for two years, 1842 and 1847, were $39.36½ and $27.50, respectively, per annum.

The number of outdoor paupers is given for several years. Usually it is small, ranging from five to ten. In 1846, however, fifty-six persons received aid outside the poorhouse. The first grant recorded was for two [dollars?] a month. The first list of outdoor paupers is for 1843 when eight persons were given aid in sums ranging from five to twenty dollars. One grant was for five dollars; four, for ten dollars; two, for fifteen dollars; and one, for twenty dollars. These allowances apparently were for a period of six months. In 1846 when outdoor relief reached the highest point for the period, the range was from five to thirty dollars for six months. Forty-one of the fifty-six received ten dollars. The last grant in 1856, to fourteen persons, shows no change in the amounts given.

The poor fund for 1832 was $1,512.22. The following, in the minutes for April 10, 1841, is interesting:

TAXES FOR THE YEAR 1839

Amount of valuation_____1,831,644 at 5c	$	915.82
Polls _____5,039 at 10c		503.90
		$1,419.72

Sheriff's commission at 6 per cent_____$ 85.18
Insolvents allowed
      1836, 165 polls_____ 16.50
      1837, 190 polls_____ 19.00
      1838, 200 polls_____ 20.00 $ 140.68

Net amount due the Court of Wardens_____$1,279.04
Paid to the Treasurer_____$700.00
Paid to the Treasurer_____ 350.86   1,050.86

Due from Sheriff to Court of Wardens_____$ 228.18

Usually the amount spent for the poorhouse is not differentiated from that spent for outdoor poor. For the year 1847, however, there was spent for the maintenance of the poorhouse $1,101.42. For the last year of the record, 1855-6, there is the following report:

      Receipts _____$3,283.23
      Expenditures _____ 2,941.64

      Balance _____$ 341.59

It was reported at the same time, however, that the court of wardens owed the superintendent of the poorhouse $745.88½.

In 1832 the salary of the superintendent of the poorhouse was fixed at $150 and it remained at that sum throughout the twenty-five years covered by this record.

The first tax for the support of the poor that appears in the record is that for 1833, ten cents on every poll and five cents on every $100 valuation of land. The highest rate recorded is a 12½ cent poll and a 7½ cent rate on land for 1852; the lowest, five cents on the poll and two and a half cents on land in 1845.

In 1848 there was the beginning of an endowment for the poorhouse. The will of Thomas D. Bennehan contained the following item: "I give to my friend, Duncan Cameron, the sum of one thousand dollars to be appropriated to Christian and benevolent purposes at his discretion." At their meeting on March 3, 1848, Cameron transferred this fund to the court of wardens, the interest to be used for the relief of the poor.

Methods of granting aid either in the poorhouse or outside do not appear to differ in any material way from those already discussed in relation to Ashe and Pasquotank counties, except that there is apparently an attempt at somewhat stricter supervision of the expenditure of the poor funds than appears in the records of the other counties. At the September meeting, 1840, for example,

Mrs. Forrest's account was submitted to the court of wardens showing how she had disbursed the allowance made for the benefit of Katy Ray which was examined and approved.

At the May meeting, 1850, it was decided that "the wardens will make no allowance for outside aid where the charge is brought without the knowledge and consent of the board," and that an announcement to this effect be placed in the *Hillsboro Recorder* and the *North Carolina Democrat*.

On August 29, 1845, it was ordered:

That hereafter applications for relief from the Wardens of the poor shall be made signed by a justice of the [peace] and two other respectable persons and that this order be published in the *Hillsboro Recorder*.

The variety of aid given and of the classes of persons receiving such aid is suggested by the following items from the record:

March, 1848. Ordered that the Superintendent pay to Henry Edwards ten dollars semiannual allowance for the support of William Moore, Esq. to October next.

April, 1851. Ordered that the Superintendent furnish Ronny Nelson with two bottles of sarsaparilla.

October, 1851. Ordered that the Superintendent pay to Hesekiah Terry the sum of $7.36 for the support of Wild Riley while he was in jail.

June, 1842. John C. Strader presented an account for attentions rendered to Amy Farrill during her confinement at a School House in his neighborhood and supporting two children for near two months of fourteen dollars which was ordered to be paid by the Superintendent.

At the April meeting, 1854, it was ordered:

That the Superintendent be authorized to purchase a milch cow at the sum of $12 for the use of Nancy Jordan in consideration that she is to keep and take care of Lucy Ellen a child of Harriett Hopkins a pauper until the first day of January 1857 free of charge to the County. Also that the Superintendent furnish her with half a barrel of corn and 20 pounds of bacon.

Children, especially afflicted children, formed a considerable group of those aided both in the poorhouse and outside. On October 1, 1832, it was ordered that Betsy Baldwin, a child in the possession of Edy Black in Hillsborough be removed to the county poorhouse. Similar orders were made at two other times within the succeeding ten years, before Betsy appeared in the list of those in that institution in 1842. In the meantime, periodical allowances for her support outside the poorhouse were being made by the wardens. Whether this and two or three other similar cases indicate an unwillingness on the part of the relatives or friends of the child to subject it to the disgrace of going to the poorhouse or to their desire to exploit the child for their own advantage is not clear.

Occasionally a child was referred to the county court to be "bound out."

The following cases are interesting. At the September, 1847, meeting the Superintendent was instructed to bring the children of Young Barbee to the poorhouse. At the November meeting of the same year the order was made

That the sum of twelve dollars and fifty cents ($12.50) be paid to C. W. Johnson, Esq. for the support of the children of Young Barbee who is at present a volunteer in the U. S. regiment in Mexico.

At the April meeting, 1848, it was ordered that twenty dollars be paid to Murrill Chesenhall for the care of the children of Young Barbee before they were brought to the poorhouse. At the same meeting the superintendent was directed to bring to the poorhouse the children of Calvin Bacon, "who is now a soldier in Mexico."

Another group cared for in the poorhouses of the period was the insane. On March 6, 1837, the wardens for Orange apointed John U. Kirkland and Cadwallader Jones to look into the propriety of erecting an additional building, a part of which was to be especially for the accommodation of lunatics. The building was completed by May of the following year. At this time it was ordered that James Gearton, "a maniac now in jail at Hillsborough," be received and placed in one of the strong rooms of the new building. It was ordered at the same time that Charles Bruce, Katy Ray, and her mother also be received. Katy Ray, however, was still outside in March, 1839.

At the November meeting, 1838, the wardens agreed to admit Nancy Strayhorn, "a deranged woman," at the rate of forty dollars a year. In 1853 the charge was raised to $75 a year.

At the March meeting, 1839, the wardens ordered that the superintendent of the poorhouse ceil the room occupied by James Gearton with plank one inch and a half thick; and on June 4th of the same year a committee was appointed to "contract for the construction of a cage for the safe-keeping of Gearton, the maniac." In December of the next year the superintendent was instructed to procure a stove for the room of Gearton and Isley.

At the September meeting, 1843, a committee was appointed to contract for the erection of a building for the accommodation of lunatic paupers. The building was to be of hewn logs, 20 feet by 26 feet, divided into four rooms, with a passage.

Insane slaves were sometimes admitted to the poorhouse. On September 5, 1853, the superintendent was instructed to receive "Ned, a deranged servant of Dr. O. F. Long." Dr. Long agreed to pay for his keep an amount equal to the average cost of keeping persons at the poorhouse. Ned, it appears, was not so insane but that he was capable of doing some work.

Aged and infirm slaves also sometimes became wards of the county. Within the period of 18 years from 1838 to 1856, ten such slaves claimed the attention of the wardens of the poor of Orange County. The following are typical entries:

May 29, 1838. Ordered that Cad Jones and James Webb be a committee to take the necessary steps to make the heirs of the late Ben Rhodes pay for the support of Betty Mintus, a slave belonging to the said estate who is now at the charge of the County at the Poor House.

It appearing to the Court of Wardens that a slave Caesar is now in this County and is liable to become chargeable to the same. It is ordered that the Secretary write to the owner of the said slave who lives in another county requesting him to take him into his possession and provide for his comfort and support.

September 2, 1850. Ordered that the Superintendent pay to Mrs. Jane Nelson $2.00 semi-annually for the maintenance of a slave of Sam C. Woods.

February 27, 1854. Ordered that the Superintendent pay E. C. Chambers the amount of his account for burying Toney, a negro, after deducting $1.50 from the amount charged for the coffin—amount $3.00.

Another group of Negroes also claimed the attention of the wardens. At the September meeting, 1856, it was ordered,

That this court recommend to the next county court to be bound to D. D. Phillips a free boy of color by the name of William James Stowers aged——years, who is to learn him the art and mystery of a coarse harness maker and shop work generally and when he arrives at the full age of twenty-one years to give him a set of tools suitable for his work and twenty-five dollars in cash or its equivalent.

There were at this time several people of this surname

in the poorhouse. This boy was probably the illegitimate child of a white mother.

Two other similar instances are recorded. In 1845
Mrs. Rebecca Gattis was notified to surrender Andrew
Jackson, a free boy of color, to the county court. In
1847 it was ordered that Calvin Ray, a free boy of color,
be bound to James Riley.

We learn little from these records about the discipline
in the early poorhouses. An occasional entry in this
record suggests that the Orange County institution was
not without its problems in this respect:

September, 1836. John Carden and Mary Helmes ran
away since the last meeting.

It is not stated whether they went together.

September, 1853. It appearing to the court that Jesse
Pearce, when able, will not work, and he being now
absent from the Poor House of his own accord, it is
Ordered, In case he will not work on his return, that
the Superintendent be, and he is hereby, directed to con-
fine him by himself, and allow him nothing but bread
and water until he is willing to work or shall consent to
leave the Poor House.
Ordered that the Superintendent give Patsy Cape and
Susan Stowers notice to look out for a home, and that he
discharge them at the end of two weeks from this day.

One closes this "Book of Proceedings of the Court of
Wardens of the County of Orange" with a good deal of
respect for these early wardens of the poor. They, as well
as the public, evidently considered the office an important
one. One is impressed by the type of men who were
elected wardens, both in the earlier period, when they
were chosen by a vote of the electors of the county, and

after 1846, when they were selected by the county court. Among the wardens were such prominent citizens as James Mebane, Esq., Col. Cadwallader Jones, Dr. James Webb, Dr. Pride Jones, and Josiah Turner.

Since these are the counties in which records of the transactions of the wardens of the poor were preserved, it is reasonable to suppose that Ashe, Duplin, Orange, and Pasquotank are representative of the counties in which one might expect to find the more businesslike and progressive methods in poor relief. In the administration of outdoor relief there is here no marked advance over the methods of relief in colonial days. There was in Pasquotank and in Orange the beginning of the poorhouse system which was partially to replace outdoor relief in nearly all the counties of the State.

In addition to these records light is sometimes thrown on methods of the administration of relief by the legislation of the period. An act for Edgecombe County, passed in 1799, provided "that from and after the passing of this act, it shall and may be lawful for the wardens of said county to let out the poor of said county, for any term not exceeding three years, in any manner they may think proper.[32]

This and other local acts indicate that a considerable degree of independence in the administration of poor relief was sometimes granted to the individual county. An act of 1817 for Northampton County, amending an earlier act, has this provision:

That the court of wardens of Northampton County,

[33] *Public Laws of North Carolina, 1799,* chap. 45.

two-thirds of the wardens being present, shall have power and they are hereby authorized to make such general bye laws, rules and regulations for the government of themselves and for receiving, letting and keeping of the parishioners as they may think proper: *Provided*, the same do not contravene the laws and constitution of the state.[33]

Three years later the powers of the wardens of this county were somewhat curtailed. The law provided that the poor were, subsequently to the passage of the act, not to be let out by the wardens in their respective districts, but as a whole at the courthouse on a specified date.[34]

Apparently the public selling of the keeping of the poor, though practised from time to time, was not the method of administering the poor funds recognized by the general law prior to 1831. Occasionally, at least, it was thought necessary to grant authority for such letting by special legislative enactment, as has already been seen in the case of Edgecombe County. For Moore County, likewise, in 1828, such a law was enacted. The following was the main provision of that act:

That instead of the mode now prescribed by law for providing for the poor in the several counties of this State, it shall be the duty of the wardens of the poor in the county of Moore, at the next May term of the Court of Pleas and Quarter Sessions for said county and at every May term of said court in each and every year thereafter, to contract with some responsible and suitable person on the lowest terms which can be obtained, to take charge of the poor of said county, whose duty it

[33] *Public Laws of North Carolina, 1817*, chap. 66.
[34] *Public Laws of North Carolina, 1820*, chap. 107.

shall be to supply the said poor with comfortable food, lodging and clothing, and to treat them in all respects with attention and humanity.[35]

That this act was interpreted to mean that the labor of the paupers should be a consideration in the contract with the person who agreed to take charge of them in this county is suggested by the supplementary act passed the next year.   This act provides:

That the wardens of the poor of Moore County are authorized and empowered to let out such of the paupers of the county as are lunatics or idiots and all helpless paupers, to suitable persons, or to contract for their support and maintenance at their own houses, as in their discretion shall seem right and proper; and nothing in said act contained shall be so construed as to require the wardens to let out this description of paupers with the other poor to a single person, or to require their personal attendance at the courthouse at the term of court when the keeping of the poor of said county is contracted for.[36]

The wardens themselves were sometimes suspected of exploiting the poor for their own financial benefit.   The following act of the General Assembly of 1829 is of interest in this connection:

Whereas the practice has sometime prevailed in Gates County for the wardens of the poor themselves to undertake to furnish the paupers with provisions and other supplies, and that owing to this the check contemplated by the law is destroyed, and supplies oftentimes furnished at rates above the market prices; for remedy whereof,
Be it enacted by the General Assembly of the State of North Carolina and it is hereby enacted by the authority of the same, That hereafter it shall not be lawful for the

[35] *Public Laws of North Carolina, 1828*, chap. 144.
[36] *Public Laws of North Carolina, 1829*, chap. 38.

wardens of the poor in Gates County to become under-
takers to furnish the paupers of said county with provisions and other supplies; but the same shall be provided
by some person or persons under contracts made with
the wardens.[37]

Sometimes it was the policy of the county upon the
building of a poorhouse to require all who received aid
from the poor funds to go there.   In 1827 an act for
Pitt County repealed a law enacted a year earlier giving
wardens discretion as to whether all the poor should be
required to live at the poorhouse.[38]   An act of 1830, on
the other hand, stated that "many cases of extreme hard-
ship have occurred in the county of Orange" because of
the requirement that all who received aid must go to the
poorhouse and gave the wardens authority to offer outdoor relief to persons who had children "unraised" and
who desired to remain with them.[39]

The usual method of selecting the superintendent of the
poorhouse in the early days of that institution in the state,
it seems, was to advertise for bids or "proposals."   This
newspaper advertisement illustrates the method:

A meeting of the Wardens of the Poor for Orange
County is requested on Wednesday of August court, at
this place, to employ a Superintendent for the Poor
House for the ensuing year, and those wishing to engage
will hand in their proposals.[40]

In 1848 Dorothea L. Dix came to the state for the purpose of arousing interest in the establishing of a state

[37] *Public Laws of North Carolina, 1829,* chap. 72.
[38] *Public Laws of North Carolina, 1827,* chap. 156.
[39] *Public Laws of North Carolina, 1830,* chap. 108.
[40] *Hillsborough Recorder,* August 17, 1825.

hospital for the insane. In gathering data for her memorial to the General Assembly she visited a large number of counties, and in the course of her investigation in these counties she went into the jails and poorhouses. Her report[41] gives a vivid picture of conditions in the poorhouse at this period. "If jails are unfit institutions for the treatment and restraint of the insane," she writes, "county poor-houses are but a degree, if at all, more suitable." The following extracts from her report throw light upon the conditions and management of these institutions in a number of counties:

The Jail of Orange is well built, and was in good order, comparing well with the best kept Jails in the State. The reverse exists in regard to the poor-house, which was neither clean nor comfortably furnished. I believe sufficient food is supplied, and in sufficient quantities. A little expenditure by the County, and a little care would render the establishment more comfortable. There were six insane there in close confinement, and much excited. The most violent, a man long a maniac and caged, was clean, but so noisy as to disturb all the premises; a large part of the time the room in which his cage was built, could be made light, but was commonly dark and close "to keep him more quiet"! A negro girl, a most pitiable case, was in the opposite building; and a white woman, also, in a separate compartment, vociferous and offensive in the extreme. In a passage between their cells or cages was a stove in which fire was maintained when necessary. The place was very offensive. The keeper could not altogether be blamed for this; he was hired to direct a poor-house, and not qualified to rule a mad-house, and should not be expected to do it.

In the Granville County poor-house is an unfortunate

[41] *North Carolina Legislative Documents, 1848-49, House of Commons Document, No. 2.*

man who for years has been chained to the floor of a wretched room; miserable and neglected, his now deformed and palsied limbs attest the severity of his sufferings through these cruel restraints; flesh and bone are crushed out of shape by the unyielding irons. He was a man of good character, industrious, frugal habits; a good citizen, and respectable as respected; be became insane, and soon the malady assumed a maniacal character: he was carried to the poor-house, loaded with chains, and left like a wild beast to live or perish; no care was bestowed to advance his recovery or to secure his comfort.

The county poor-house establishment [of Caswell County], not distant from Yanceyville, consists of a series of decent one story buildings, kept remarkably clean and neat, and reflecting credit at once upon the county, and those who have the immediate charge. Of the four insane residents here two were in close confinement: a woman in a room of sufficient size who was in a highly excited state. The insane man was in a sort of stall or cage, and at the season of my visit to the place was clean. The noise, perversity, and bad habits of these unfortunate persons was a source of much disquiet in the establishment.

The [Rockingham County] poor-house, but a short distance from Wentworth, is singularly neat, and well-ordered; the inmates sufficiently well-clad and very neat and respectable. The buildings require repairs. The house is well kept, but more comforts might well be supplied.

The [Stokes County] poor-house, about three miles from Germanton, is extremely comfortless, the apartments are entirely too much crowded, and the arrangements are not suited to promote the comfort or good order of the inmates. . . . Rooms of the poor are all ill-furnished and out of repair. Residence of the Superintendent very neat and comfortable. There was one insane woman then at liberty but often confined in a cell, in all respects unfit for one in her condition. I cannot forbear the remark, that when not in close confinement, she was very improperly situated in the room she occupied.

There were several others in the house in a demented state.

The poor-house [of Surry County] is about three miles from Rockford, the Superintendent resides in town, and keeps several negroes to look after the poor, of whom there were in September, about thirty. There were no insane in close confinement, but two who were allowed the freedom of the place.

[In Guilford County] the old poor-house several miles from Greensboro is about to be abandoned, being utterly comfortless and out of repair. New buildings on the Hillsboro road are nearly completed, and there is no doubt that the establishment will be in all respects well-ordered and fitly conducted.

The [Davidson] County poor-house about six miles from Lexington was pretty well ordered, but too little visited. The supplies of food and clothing seemed sufficient for both health and comfort: but there, as elsewhere, the insane were out of place and in a bad state. For this no blame is to be attached to the superintendent, so far as I could judge. One very crazy man was chained to his bedstead; he was noisy, filthy, and truly repulsive. A crazy woman, but quiet, was rolled in a quantity of soiled bed clothing. . . . Besides these there were two demented patients.

The [Rowan County] poor-house about two miles from Salisbury, requires so much to render it comfortable that it would be difficult to know how to enumerate its deficiencies: the house occupied by the keeper was quite the most comfortless abode that I have seen in North Carolina, except repairs, certainly not habitable for the winter. No insane man in confinement in this institution.

The [Iredell] County poor-house, a few miles from Statesville is situated in a singularly secluded spot, remote from supervision and often observation, and is a model of neatness, comfort, and good order; having a most efficient master and mistress, especially the latter, upon whose cares in these institutions by far the most is dependent. All in all, this was in much the best condition of any poor-house I have seen in North Carolina, neat, plain, and decent, it would do credit to any State; but it is no fit place for the insane. Since I was there in September, a highly respected citizen writes me that a young woman has been sent to the poor-house so violently insane that it is quite unfit she should remain there. Also a man has in that county, very recently become so violently mad as to be quite unmanageable, and having no Hospital in the State, they have confined him with *chains and manacles, hand and feet,* and do the best they can.

Of Wilkes County it is recorded:

There is no poor-house in this County.

The [Burke] County poor-house, about three miles from Morganton, is not well situated; the buildings are out of repair, and ill-arranged within for either comfort or convenience in times of sickness or of health. I should think that the Superintendent was kind and faithful in the discharge of all his duties toward the poor. Here as at most of the poor-houses in North Carolina religious services are frequently holden.

There is no county poor-house in or near Marion, [McDowell County.]

Formerly there was a county poor-house six or seven miles from Asheville [Buncombe County], but its remote situation and serious discomforts through bad management led to the entire breaking up of the establishment some time since. A plan succeeded this, somewhat original, which when I was in Asheville, had not been fully carried into effect; having no perception of its merits and claims to commendation, I shall dwell but slightly upon the subject, merely stating on authority of several of the citizens, that it was considered in constructing the new jail, expedient to make it of sufficient capacity to accommodate at one and the same time and place, the vagrants and felons of the county, and the unfortunate poor. The enclosed yard, "at present unimproved," is of sufficient extent to permit the erection of additional buildings "if needed." "It is believed," said my informant, "that the wardens and overseers consult economy by this arrangement in various ways, especially as one man can keep the prisoners and the poor, saving the cost of hiring a second individual for the latter service." But one pauper has been sent to jail, and he ran away, dissatisfied with his quarters, in about three weeks.

The [Rutherford] County poor-house, a short distance from Rutherfordton, is not so comfortable as respects the buildings and furnishings as it should be made. The Superintendent seemed a favorite of the poor there.

The [Cleveland] County poor-house, about three miles from Shelby, is a small but neatly kept, and seemingly comfortable establishment. It seems to me that the Superintendent received an insufficient recompense for the difficult charge the situation of several of the inmates involved.

The [Lincoln County] poor-house, several miles from Lincolnton, had but three inmates in October; their condition was uniformly represented as not good, and the establishment described as being objectionable. Perceiving influential citizens prompt to admit existing evils, I did not personally visit it.

No poor-house in or near Dallas [Gaston County]; but one such needed for the County poor. Several insane in the County.

The [Mecklenburg] County poor-house, several miles from Charlotte, was nearly deserted in October, having but two of the County poor; a partially insane woman and a paralytic man.

The [Cabarrus] County poor-house, about two and a half miles from Concord, is very deficient in means for promoting the comfort of the infirm inmates. In a miserably dilapidated out-building, perhaps ten feet square, open on all sides to the ingress of the winds, rain, and snow, I found a crazy man chained to the floor, filthy and disgusting.

There is no poor-house in or near Albemarle, [Stanly County].

The [Montgomery] County poor-house, at Lawrenceville, requires, it appears to me, much more careful attention on the part of the wardens, to supply comfortable and necessary attendance upon the aged and infirm, who alone occupy the buildings. Nothing could be more creditable to these feeble women than the neatness and care with which they kept their apparel and their apartments.

The [Moore] County poor-house, not distant from Carthage, was excellently kept by a conscientious and kindhearted family, to whose cares the comforts of the inmates are ascribable, rather than to the provision made by county officials. The buildings are much out of repair and unfit for winter habitation, or for stormy days at any season. The custom so worthy of entire condemnation, that of selling off the poor in mass, by lots or singly, to the lowest bidders exists in Moore County. The poor are fed, clothed, supplied with bed clothing, and fuel and waited on at the rate of *eight cents the day each;* a sum which cannot pay those who undertake this charge. That I found the poor well supplied with food and well clad, I repeat was certainly ascribable to the liberality and Christianity of the present keepers, rather than to the just guardianship of the public.

The [Cumberland] County poor-house within three miles of Fayetteville is well situated, and apparently excellently kept: cleanliness, that crowning excellence in house-keeeping, prevailed in every room save one, and I imagine might with the exercise of sufficient determination, be secured even in that. In a log building, well constructed, and admitting sufficient light and air, planned so as to be warmed in damp and cold weather were two small apartments for the insane: at the time I was there one room was vacant, the other was occupied by a violently excited and noisy insane man, whose shouts and vociferations reached me at a distance from the poor-house.

[In Sampson County] the county poor are said to be well clothed and supplied with wholesome food.

[In Duplin] the wardens of the county poor-house

which is situated east of Warsaw, several miles from
Kenansville, have the reputation of giving uncommon
attention to the temporal and spiritual comforts and con-
solations of the poor. Religious services are holden at the
poor-house. At present there are no insane persons there.

The [New Hanover] County poor-house on the confines
of Wilmington is in a miserable dilapidated condition;
fallen wholly from its former well-deserved reputation
of being one of the best Institutions for the poor in the
country. Apparently the acting wardens are responsible
for its decline.

The [Wayne] County poor-house, several miles from
Goldsboro, seemed quite decently kept, and in many
respects bore an air of comfort. There seemed to be
neglect from abroad in the attendance upon the sick;
several individuals were evidently suffering from want of
medical advice and prescription. This establishment is
but seldom visited, and the comforts enjoyed seemed
chiefly referable to the care of the occupants. One of the
poor, an insane man, had wandered away: an insane
woman was so far controllable as to be steadily and
usefully occupied.

Of Lenoir County it is recorded only that the poor of
the county are not numerous by comparison with the ad-
jacent country.

The [Craven] County poor-house, a short distance
from Newbern is well situated, and has the reputation
of being well kept in general. The keeper's house, and
several rooms occupied by the poor, were neat and well-
ordered; others were in poor condition. A sunday school
is taught here by persons from Newbern, whose
Christianity is illustrated in their practice of its precepts.

The [Beaufort] County poor-house not distant from
Washington, and reached over a good road, is pleasantly
situated, but in a spot well known for its unhealthiness,
having been abandoned by the former owner of the property for its liability, to create fevers, and for the general
insalubrity of the place. Offering at first glance the appearance of a comfortable institution, it fails to show

forth either private or public efficient and fit direction. The sick and the children certainly suffer; and those able to work need a director to insist upon their action. I found one woman here insane, but quiet.

Of Pitt County it is said that the poor are well cared for.

I did not visit the poor-house of this county [Edge-combe] established some distance from Tarboro, but it bears a good reputation.

The poor-house [of Halifax County] nearly three miles from Halifax, has much need of competent care, and efficient superintendence. Most of the inmates are aged and infirm. The buildings are well situated and conveniently planned for the occupants; but deficiently furnished, except one room furnished by the individual who dwells in it. The sick need nursing, care, and comforts; and all require supervision.

The [Northampton County] poor-house, a mile and a half from Jackson, consists of five dilapidated, unfurnished rooms, at present abandoned. The Superintendent who resides in a pleasantly situated, comfortable house, distributed quarterly to one hundred beneficiaries an allowance of meat, meal, and clothing, at a cost to the county of about $2,500.

The [Nash County] poor-house I had not time to visit, but understand it is comfortable.

Of the thirty-six counties included in Miss Dix's report, thirty-two maintained poorhouses. In fifteen of these conditions are set down as bad. In ten of those actually visited conditions are called good. Three others had good reputations. In eleven of the institutions visited insane inmates were found. The total number of insane inmates reported was eighteen. Some of these were violently insane, and had to be confined in cages or by chaining. The total number of inmates is given in only a very few instances. In these cases it is surprisingly large.

Miss Dix was interested primarily in the condition of the insane in the poorhouses. She had for several years been engaged in studying the condition of the insane in various states. Unfavorable conditions as they affected this class could hardly escape her attention. The proportion of insane found in these institutions by her was scarcely greater than that found in the county homes at the present. The proportion of violently insane was greater; but as late as 1922 the State Board of Charities and Public Welfare found insane inmates of county homes chained to the floor.[42] Many county homes, among the number some of the newest and most modern plants, still have apartments for the confinement of the insane who cannot be treated as ordinary inmates.

Aside from its attention to the insane the Dix report is very much like all subsequent reports. Some of the poorhouses were comfortable living places; others were wholly lacking in comforts. Often there was indifference on the part of those charged with general supervision of the poor; or there was incompetency and apparent carelessness on the part of those in immediate charge of the poorhouses.

At the beginning of the period under consideration, the administration of the poor funds was transferred from the vestries to similar bodies called overseers of the poor, elected by a vote of the freemen of the county as the vestrymen had been elected by a vote of the freeholders of the parish. These overseers of the poor were to select from their own number two wardens of the poor,

[42] North Carolina State Board of Charities and Public Welfare, *Biennial Report, 1920-22*, p. 46.

as the vestrymen had formerly selected two churchwardens, who should have active charge of the relief
of the poor. Later the power of selecting the wardens of
the poor was transferred to the county court of pleas
and quarter sessions made up of the justices of the peace
of the county. The power of levying a tax for the poor
was also transferred to the county court. The law of 1793
had authorized the wardens of the poor to build almshouses. By 1831 this power, too, had been transferred to
the court of pleas and quarter sessions.

The period saw the development of a definite statement of the law of legal settlement, adapted from the
English law of the Elizabethan period, bringing it to the
form that was to be retained to the present time.

The period saw also the development of the poorhouse
in North Carolina. As the relief of the poor by public
funds had been very slowly accepted as a general policy
in colonial days and the early years of independence,
so now the idea of taxing themselves to build houses for
the care of the poor had to be repeatedly presented before
it was accepted as a part of the general policy of county
government. But finally after half a century of legislation on the subject, it was so accepted.

There were those, however, who saw the need for a
radically different policy in dealing with the problem
of the poor, and the period was not without suggestions
looking toward the prevention of poverty. The most interesting proposal along this line was the well known
Murphey report in advocacy of a public school system.
Tuition in the public schools was to be free to only a

limited group of pupils selected from the poor to be educated at State expense.[43] The proposal failed of approval, and when a public school system was finally inaugurated in 1841 no mention was made in the law of the education of the poor. For many years, however, the stigma of being in the public mind "charity schools" retarded the development of the public schools of the state.

Poverty continued throughout the period to be associated in public opinion with idleness and petty crime. The almshouses were frequently designated in the laws "poor- and work-houses," and provision was made for the commitment of misdemeanants as well as the poor to these institutions.

[43] W. H. Hoyt, editor, *The Papers of Archibald D. Murphey*, (*Publications of the North Carolina Historical Commission*, 1914).

CHAPTER IV

POOR RELIEF BY THE BOARDS OF COUNTY
COMMISSIONERS, 1868-1919

THE constitution of 1868 transferred the control of
county affairs, including the support of the poor, from
the courts of pleas and quarter sessions to the boards of
county commissioners, which were created the central
governing bodies in the several counties.[1] Chapter 20,
section 24, of the *Public Laws of 1868*, carrying the constitutional mandate into effect, made it the duty of the
county commissioners

to provide for the maintenance, and do all such matters
and things as they deem expedient, for the comfort and
well-ordering of the poor; to employ biennially, by
public letting or otherwise, some competent person as
overseer of the poor; to institute proceedings by warrant
of their chairman against any person coming into the
county, who is likely to become chargeable thereto and to
cause the removal of such person to the county where he
was last legally settled; and to recover by action in the
Superior Court from said county, all the charges and
expenses whatever incurred for the maintenance or removal of such person.

Eight years later it was provided by law that

No pauper shall be let out at public auction, but the
board of commissioners may make such arrangement for
the support of paupers with their friends or other persons,
when not maintained at the county home for the aged
infirm, as may be deemed best.[2]

[1] *Constitution of North Carolina*, art. VIII, sec. 1.
[2] *Public Laws of North Carolina, 1876-77*, chap. 277, sec. 2;
Consolidated Statutes of North Carolina, 1341.

This continued without important change to be the law until 1915, when an act was passed providing "that section 1318 of the Revisal of 1905 be and the same is hereby amended by striking out in sub-section fourteen in line two after the word 'biennially' and before the word 'some' the words 'by public letting or otherwise,' "[3] which being interpreted means that since 1915, by virtue of this act, there has been no legal sanction for the ancient custom, still followed by several counties, of letting the keeping of the county home to the lowest responsible bidder. In 1891 an attempt had been made to remove the stigma implied in the name by enacting that the county institution for the care of the poor no longer should be known as the "poorhouse," but should be "designated and provided for as 'the home for the aged and infirm.' "[4]

From time to time the position of the county home and the powers and duties of the boards of county commissioners have been defined by the Supreme Court of the state. This tribunal, for instance, has declared that providing for a county home is a necessary expense.[5] This gives the commissioners the authority to issue bonds for the building of a new county home without submitting the proposition to a vote of the people. It is not mandatory, however, that the commissioners provide a county home of any kind. The law imposes the general duty to provide for the poor. The place, method, and extent of relief is left to the judgment and discretion of the

[3] *Public Laws of North Carolina, 1915*, chap. 274.

[4] *Public Laws of North Carolina, 1891*, chap. 138.

[5] Commissioners *vs.* Spitzer, *North Carolina Supreme Court Reports*, vol. 173, p. 147.

4. Better Types of County Homes Built Two Decades Ago

Iredell County Home

county commissioners.[6] But it is the exclusive right of the legislature to determine and declare by whom and how the indigent of the state entitled to support shall be ascertained and from what fund and by whom allowances for their support shall be made.[7]

When the constitutional convention of 1868 met, the movement toward the creation of state agencies for supervision and standardization of poor relief and of other charities was already under way in several of the more progressive states of the Union. Massachusetts had taken the lead by the creation of a Board of State Charities in 1863. She had been followed in 1867 by Ohio and New York. Illinois, Pennsylvania, and Rhode Island were about to create similar boards. This spirit of reform abroad in the land found expression in North Carolina in a most progressive article in the new constitution, dealing with charities and corrections.

Among the delegates to the constitutional convention was Reverend G. W. Welker of Guilford County. As a young man Mr. Welker had come to the state from Pennsylvania in 1841 and had immediately entered the ministry of the German Reformed Church, in which he was for many years a leader. When the convention met, Mr. Welker was made chairman of the committee to whom was entrusted the drafting of the article of the constitution dealing with "punishments, penal institutions, and public charities." The enlightened report of

[6] Copple vs. Commissioners, North Carolina Supreme Court Reports, vol. 138, p. 132.

[7] Board vs. Commissioners, North Carolina Supreme Court Reports, vol. 113, p. 379.

this committee, which became Article XI of the constitution, provided among other things that the General Assembly at its first session following the adoption of the
constitution should "appoint and define the duties of
a board of public charities, to whom shall be entrusted
the supervision of all charitable and penal State institutions and who shall annually report to the Governor upon
their condition, with suggestions for their improvement."[8]

The General Assembly at the session of 1868-9, carrying this constitutional mandate into effect, created and
elected a State Board of Public Charities. Early in
1870 the Board presented its first report. In the months
preceding the report it had made a rather careful survey
of conditions in poorhouses. Dr. G. W. Blacknall, a
member of the board, visited a number of counties. The
secretary, W. J. Palmer, principal of the state school for
the deaf and the blind, sent a questionnaire to the
boards of county commissioners of the various counties.
Replies were received from all the counties except six.
In the report of the State Board the chairman, Rev. G.
William Welker, says in regard to the poorhouses:

The County Alms-houses are also an institution of the
olden time, and very properly called "Poor Houses."
These are the receptacles of the infirm, aged and
diseased who are destitute or cast off by unnatural or
equally poor kindred, the orphan and the child of
poverty, for whom beats no heart warm with the kindly
emotions. Here is almost equal banishment from the
presence of human love and care, as in the case of the
prison. The respectable, aged and infirm pauper is shut
up with the wornout strumpet, whose very presence is

[8] *Constitution of North Carolina*, art. XI, sec. 7.

pollution, and no care is had, in many cases, for the innocence of childhood. Perhaps, at rare intervals, a sermon is preached at the "Poor House," but no provision is made for teaching the children gathered there, or the religious instruction of any of its inmates. The State appears satisfied with the knowledge that there is a Poor House—that there is an annual tax imposed upon the citizens which is in some manner supposed to advantage the poor. No enlightened Christian concern is felt for the welfare and comfort of these forlorn creatures, or for the education and training of the neglected children of want, who know nothing of the blessedness of parental affection. Something more is surely demanded of a Christian State than what is now done in these institutions . . . to provide for the infirm and poor properly. The whole system, or rather want of system that seems to have grown up by accident and without any benevolent concern for the welfare of the pauper classes, . . . needs patient and thorough revision.[9]

A further glimpse at the poorhouse population is afforded by his discussion of the provision in the new constitution for the training of the "idiotic" and "mentally imbecile." Of these classes he says:

Thousands have been, many are even now, cast into that common receptacle, the County Poor House, where amid filth and neglect they do not live but only languish out the burden of an existence that is scarcely more than physical.[10]

In this same report Dr. G. W. Blacknall, who as special agent of the board of charities had visited a number of poorhouses, writes:

[9] *Report of North Carolina State Board of Public Charities,* 1870, p. 7.
[10] *Ibid.,* p. 12.

Of our poor houses I will first speak, and I trust you will excuse me when I say, in most cases, they are really what their name indicates—poor houses—yes, poor houses. Most of them are not only a disgrace to the State, but a sin against humanity; and to make them what they should be, a radical change must be brought about. To speak of their many imperfections gives me no pleasure, and I am sure would be a mortification to you. Suffice it to say, the houses are fast coming to decay, not sufficient in size and number, and, in many cases, no better than out doors—and the bedding and clothes are in a bad condition, and the inmates generally a miserable set of people, left there to eke out an unhappy existence.[11]

He found many insane in the poorhouses.[12]

The replies to Mr. Palmer's questionnaire brought a fund of interesting information. Six counties, as has already been said, failed to report. Six counties—Ashe, Buncombe, Clay, Onslow, Transylvania, and Watauga—had no poorhouses. Yancey was just building. In Yadkin "the poorhouse having become destitute of furniture, the poor were put with different persons through the county. The commissioners anticipate refurnishing it, and taking the poor back at an early date. About fifty persons receive help from the county at present, but only about one-half of these will be admitted into the poor house." There were no inmates in the Sampson poorhouse. The poor, according to the report, were provided for in each township. In the cases of eight poorhouses it was stated that the buildings were of logs. In one case there were one brick building and three "wooden" buildings. In many cases it was simply stated that the buildings were

[11] *Ibid.*, p. 103.
[12] *Ibid.*, p. 109.

"wood." It is probable that some of these were of logs. The term "double-building" used in several instances especially suggests log buildings. Four counties reported brick buildings. Nine thousand ninety-three acres were reported as belonging to the poor farms. Of this land 1,122 acres were in cultivation. In three instances the land was called "good." Usually the quality was said to be "poor" or "very poor"; occasionally, "fair" or "common." These county homes housed 1,097 inmates. In Clay and Onslow counties the keeping of the poor was let to the lowest bidder. In Wilkes one inmate had been punished by "chaining and whipping" for abusing the rest of the paupers. Salaries of superintendents ranged from board for self and family to five hundred dollars a year. One county—Bladen—paid its superintendent five hundred dollars. One paid four hundred. One paid four hundred for the superintendent and a horse. Four paid two hundred to two hundred and fifty dollars. Nine paid less than two hundred. One gave the superintendent board for himself and his family. The other counties paid a specified amount for each inmate per day, per month, or per year. These amounts ranged from three dollars per month to six and a half. Usually, perhaps in all cases, the keeper had the use of the farm in addition to the money paid him. The cost per week per inmate as given ranged from fifty cents to four dollars. One dollar to one dollar and fifty cents is the modal range.[13]

Such is a picture of the poorhouse in North Carolina

[13] *Report North Carolina State Board of Public Charities, 1870,* pp. 90-94.

in 1869. This, it is true, was just after the close of the Civil War and in the midst of the reconstruction period, when the State was impoverished, disorganized, and thoroughly weakened in civic morale; but conditions in county almshouses do not appear greatly different from those of 1849 or of 1889 or of 1919.

In 1872 the Board of Public Charities appointed Dr. C. T. Murphy, who had succeeded Rev. G. W. Welker as its president, to visit as many as possible of the county institutions. The report says that

quite a number of counties were visited and the poor houses and jails examined as thoroughly as possible; these counties were in the western, central, and eastern portions of the State, giving, it is believed a fair average of the accommodations and treatment of the paupers and prisoners of the State.

In most of the western counties the poor houses were found to be mere hovels, built of logs and daubed with clay or lined with split boards, some low, leaky, and badly decayed both in the roofs and floors; some filthy; but few cleanly or at all comfortable. In the more central and eastern counties frame tenements were generally occupied, and of these only the overseers' buildings and occasionally not even these were either comfortable, cleanly, or at all suited to purposes of an almshouse. In brief, the poor houses as a class are properly and appropriately named—they are "poor houses" indeed. The bedsteads and bedding are in keeping with the houses, old and dilapidated; the bed clothes and mattresses so filthy and loathsome as to suggest the idea of a sort of poor house *hydrophobia*, and greatly deficient of even hay or straw, and instances were noticed where, on account of want of clothing, the inmates were compelled to cut up the ticking of their mattresses for the purpose of covering their nakedness. This condition of things was found to exist in counties where clover, hay, and all the grasses are successfully cultivated, and prosperity and plenty in other respects prevails.

In two or three counties only were brick houses found; in one of these the floors were badly decayed, and in only one did we find a building well suited to the purposes of an almshouse; this was in the county of Guilford, and was erected under the supervision of that noble patriot and statesman, ex-Gov. Morehead, who, in this respect as well as others, was far in advance of his State and times. . . .

We found some sort of medical attention allowed by most of the County Boards, but was let out generally by contract to the lowest bidder, and awarded sometimes to incompetent men. In certain counties this *poor boon* was denied even where the inmates suffered severely with both acute and chronic diseases. In one county we found in a filthy room a woman, suffering with an extensive scrofulous ulcer covering almost the entire neck, shoulders and side of the face, and emitting the most insupportable effluvia, was domiciled in the same room with an aged paralytic unable to raise himself in bed, and no treatment was afforded either, and no physician had visited them in the poor house for over two years.

We found but in two counties medicines kept in the poor house, and no such thing as a dispensary or any room set apart for the physician where he could weigh or dispense the medicines needed by the inmates. It is needless to state to any one ever within the wards of a hospital, the importance of this arrangement.

As a class we found the overseers either *imbeciles* or soulless mercenaries, taking the positions at prices so ruinously low as to preclude the possibility of fair dealing or honest provision for the inmates, their greatest anxiety appearing to be to keep on satisfactory terms with the County Boards. From 11 to 16 cents per day, with the privilege of working the inmates on the poor and unproductive farms, was allowed for their support. Only in *one* county visited we found the keeper charged with harsh treatment or of requiring the paupers to labor on the farms when unable to do so. In this instance the County commissioners stipulated to furnish support, and allowed the overseer the proceeds of the farm, by which it was claimed he realized over fifteen hundred dollars per annum profit. This being the only conspicuous instance of an energetic overseer, and being in such striking contrast with those so indolent and inefficient, we were inclined to look upon him with favor and commendation.

In another county visited, upon well-grounded suspicion, corroborated by reliable information, we became satisfied that the keeper of the poor house was so infamously base and vile as to be living in almost open adultery with some of the female inmates under his care, thus prostituting his position, which should have been humane and sacred, to that of licentiousness and libertinism.

In one county it was found that by written consent of the County Commissioners a marriage had been permitted between pauper inmates, the one a confirmed male epileptic of fifteen years standing with a scrofulously blind woman, young enough to give promise of an imbecile and effete off-spring.

Who, that ever passed through the wards of an insane asylum, even the best regulated hospital, for the care and keeping of this pitiable class, but who has had his heart crushed into gloomy sadness and his tenderest sympathies aroused for these afflicted, forlorn and helpless creatures, will not say to himself, "God grant it may never be thus with me or mine," and reason again with himself and wonder if all these mind-lost fellow beings are treated humanely, kindly and gently, and think how cruel indeed it would be to neglect them or injure them or treat them harshly? and with these feelings welling up in his soul, let us ask him to go with us (if he pleases) to the county poor house and walk with us through *these wards,* and he will perhaps see an epileptic that, by the often recurring convulsions the brain has sustained so many shocks, has lost reason and intelligence— driven out and are gone forever. In another corner is the poor old paralytic, crying for some one to raise him up to enable him to slake his thirst with cold water, or to partake of his scanty meal. Just beyond is the idiot, with his vacant stare and tattered clothing; and a little further back, in a closeted corner, you hear loud cries, with pelting and banging against the walls, alternate cries and laughs, imprecations and song. Look into this little nook of a cell, and you see the shivering naked form of an insane man or woman whom the keeper will tell you will not wear clothes, nor have bedding, nor even straw upon which to lie, who is sometimes violent, and breaking out, nearly crush to death some poor blind man, woman or child. No skillful physician is here to prescribe even a palliative dose to soothe and compose the irritable nervous system; no quiet chamber to be left alone to sleep; no careful watching—all is blissful ignorance, disorder and confusion.

This is indeed a sad picture, but true to life, of our poor houses this day. . . .

It was found where the County Boards furnished provisions there seemed to be no complaint as to the quantity of food, but where the commissioners had let out to the lowest bidder contracts with keepers at from 10 to 15 cents per day for entire keeping and support, there was not a sufficient quantity allowed, and no care taken as to variety or healthfulness of food. In fact, we can state, with the fewest exceptions, the food provided for the poor is almost universally the same throughout the State, viz: *"Baltimore bulk bacon,"* and badly cooked Indian corn bread. In a few of the wheat growing counties wheat bread was used more frequently, but even west of the mountains, the home of the grasses—a land, it may be said, flowing with milk and honey—beef, mutton, chickens, eggs, cheese, milk, flour, etc., etc. (in fact everything is produced in abundance) we found that this same *Baltimore bulk bacon* had been ordered by the economical and provident commissioners, and at heavy expense had been hauled over the mountains from the east to supply the poor with *green salt meat,* when their own local markets were glutted with all the richest, fattest, cheapest fresh meats, and every business man complaining that the great want of that section was the means of rail transportation for the immense quantities of agricultural products of almost every name and description known as products of the temperate zone.

If it be possible to contemplate any one feature more than another of the faulty management of our poor houses, it is in the neglect and want of proper cultivation of vegetable gardens. About an acre is usually fenced off for this purpose, and if properly cultivated and fertilized, as could easily be done by one of fair intelligence and energy, full half support could be produced; but as found to exist, barely sufficient is produced for the overseer and his family, and apples and fruits during their season (so abundant the past year in North Carolina) was regarded as a great luxury by the inmate poor, and was seldom found among them either as a relish or food.

By personal inquiry, it was ascertained that the County Boards in many counties had manifested some anxiety as to the best means of caring for their poor, and would frankly acknowledge that their best efforts had not been as successful as they desired, but seldom could be persuaded that better treatment could be instituted without the expenditure of increased sums of money. Occupying as they do the responsible and thankless position of adjuncts between the tax-payers and the pauper, the treasurer and disburser were and are placed in a dilemma between the two; not able to please both, they yield generally to the stronger influence, and decide with the thoughtless majority to stint a little further the paupers and their keepers; and some heartless, soulless man, without energy, industry or character will always be found to accept the situation at a little less than his predecessor, expecting by hook or by crook to make up his losses out of the helpless paupers under his control.

In some counties a sadder picture still presents itself; the County Commissioners seem to know nothing about the poor house or its inmates only through the reports and

representations of the overseer or by hearsay. Neither
they nor the judges, grand juries, physicians, nor any
county official whatever, visits this forsaken abode, and
know nothing of the real conditions of the poor inmates.
As a result of this indifference many abuses are found to
exist, such, in brief, as the want of the proper separation of sexes and classification of inmates. At present
there is no discrimination of age, sex, condition, but all
are heterogeneously and indiscriminately thrown
together.

We noticed male insane persons in a state of entire
nudity walking among the women and children, around
and in their various wards, and were informed that it was
of common occurrence, and many others, male and female
insane, were confined in small rooms, resembling mere
bleak and comfortless cages for brutes, and not one
solitary effort made towards providing for their comfort or cure.[14]

Again the Civil War and Reconstruction may be offered as explanations of the conditions described in this
report; but on many items this report of 1872 is so
similar to that of 1922[15] that one wonders whether
economic conditions had much more to do with conditions
described in the earlier report than with those discussed
by the State Board of Charities and Public Welfare at
the later date.

Indifferent to public welfare as a function of the
state, hostile to a program inaugurated by "radicals,"
under a grueling poverty that furnished a plausible excuse for leaving undone anything which its people were
not interested in doing, the state allowed the Board of

[14] *North Carolina Legislative Documents, 1872-3*, Document 22.
[15] North Carolina State Board of Charities and Public Welfare,
Biennial Report, 1920-22, pp. 40, 43, 46, 54-57.

Public Charities to cease to function, first through the withholding by the legislature of the meager appropriation granted at the time of its creation, and then through the failure of the Governor to fill vacancies on the board as they occurred by the expiration of the terms of the members. From 1873 to 1889, therefore, we have no official reports as to poor relief and no official records except such as appear in the minute books of the boards of county commissioners, the financial records of county treasurers, and some meager records, usually not extending over many years, of admissions to county almshouses, kept by the superintendents. In 1889, however, the State Board of Public Charities was revived, and in 1891 it published a brief report for the years 1889 and 1890.

The new board was given no means to make inspections or investigations or even to print blank forms upon which to obtain statistical reports from the counties. Its first report, therefore, is confined to state institutions and such county institutions as happened to be near the homes of various members of the State Board. Among these are five county almshouses, the official name of which had by this time been changed from "County Poor House" to "County Home for the Aged and Infirm." The first of these is Buncombe County's institution. This county, after the experiment of using the county jail for housing its poor as a measure of economy, as reported by Miss Dix in 1849, and a period with no almshouse, during which the poor were given a small amount of outdoor relief—one dollar a month to each person in 1869—now had two wooden buildings, one, one hundred and sixty-eight feet by fourteen feet, and the

other, fifty-six feet by fourteen feet, both of one story, and
containing respectively fourteen and four rooms. There
were thirty-four inmates. Chatham was reported as having framed houses, but in the next biennial report the
houses were said to be of logs; so probably we have
here the same plant as in 1869. Craven had increased
the number of her buildings from four to seven within
the twenty years. The number of inmates had decreased
from thirty-seven to twenty-one. Granville in 1869 had
four brick cottages with two rooms each and one wooden
building with one room. By 1889 the wooden building
had given place to a fifth two-roomed brick building.
The number of inmates had decreased six in twenty
years. The institution was reported well kept. Wake had
added one to its group of two-roomed wooden cottages.
The buildings were reported "cleanly and well ordered."
The county workhouse was "within the same enclosure,
but separated by broken ground." The county home
housed sixty-four inmates as compared with fifty-six in
1869.[16]

During the next biennial period the secretary of the
State Board of Public Charities, Captain C. B. Denson,
organized in the various counties committees,[17] called in
the records sometimes boards of visitors and sometimes
county boards of charities. The duties of these voluntary
committees were to visit the county institutions and to

[16] North Carolina State Board of Public Charities, *Biennial Report, 1889-90*, p. 6.
[17] North Carolina State Board of Public Charities, *Biennial Report, 1891-92*, pp. 7-8.

make such reports concerning them as might be requested by the State Board.

The biennial report for 1891-1892 contains reports from fifty-six of the ninety-six counties for the year 1891 [18] and reports from nearly all of them for 1892.[9] Unfortunately the 1892 reports do not contain information on all the items included in the 1869 report and therefore do not lend themselves so well to comparison as the less complete (so far as number of counties is concerned) reports of 1891. In his introduction to the report the secretary says:

There is . . . much of encouragement to every lover of humanity in the good work that has been done throughout the commonwealth during the past year. Not a few reports exhibit evidence of the hand of reform already. New "homes" are being built, old ones repaired, unfaithful officials dismissed, inquiry set on foot in regard to others, and a spirit of awakening justice to the afflicted and helpless everywhere manifested. But there is a great field of investigation, and your efforts are invoked by our best informed citizens in cases where local applications and complaints have been unavailing. . . .

I beg to call your attention to two questions of importance. One of these is the disposition of veteran Confederate soldiers now in county "homes," . . . The other question pertains to the proper support, education and management of eighty-one children reported to be now living in the poor-houses or homes of the several counties (fifty-six only reported), not a few of whom were actually born there.[20]

He then proposes that the old soldiers might be trans-

[18] *Ibid.*, p. 120.
[19] *Ibid.*, p. 270.
[20] *Ibid.*, p. 9.

ferred to the Soldiers' Home "when its capacity allows their admission," and that the "Children's Home" of Buncombe County may suggest a way to care for the children.[21] The next year, however, one hundred and fourteen children were reported in county homes.[22]

The detailed reports from the boards of visitors of the various counties show improvement, indeed, but give no cause for great enthusiasm about conditions in these institutions. Thirteen county homes now had brick buildings. One of these was the Person County Home which in 1921, thirty years later, had wooden cottages, some of them of logs. Seven counties still used log buildings. Among these was Iredell, whose poorhouse in 1849 Miss Dix pronounced the best in the state and one which would be a credit to any state. Yadkin reported framed buildings. It now (1927) has log buildings. Salaries of keepers had risen somewhat. One county, Wake, now paid its keeper six hundred dollars a year. He, however, also had charge of the workhouse in which were housed the prisoners worked on the roads. Three other counties paid four hundred dollars or more; five, three hundred dollars; and six, two hundred to two hundred and fifty dollars. In 1869, 1,097 inmates were reported; in 1892, 1,192, an increase in the twenty-two years of ninety-three. In twenty-six counties there was a decrease in the number of inmates.

While salaries of superintendents had advanced somewhat, the cost of maintenance in the average home was lower than in 1869. The weekly cost per inmate ranged

[21] *Ibid.*, p. 10.
[22] *Ibid.*, p. 289.

from twenty-five cents to two dollars and twenty-five cents. In half a dozen of the fifty-six counties reporting, the cost was two dollars or more. In an equal number it was less than one dollar. The others fell between one and two dollars, the two largest groups being one dollar and twenty-five cents and one dollar and fifty cents. The methods of farming evidently had not changed materially. Eighteen counties reported no live stock of any kind on the county home farm. In nine other cases where live stock was enumerated there were no horses, mules, or oxen. In twelve instances there was one horse or mule. Only a small portion of the land, usually described as poor, was in cultivation.[23] A few extracts from, and summaries of, reports from the counties will throw additional light on conditions in the county homes at this period.

Buncombe County. "No system of outdoor relief; all persons needing such aid required to go to Home, unless it be exceptional case; but about 50 persons outside Home receive $3 per month." A sizable number of exceptional cases, one thinks.

Cabarrus County. "We are convinced that the food for the inmates of the home could and should be better. And there certainly should be some provision made for providing the sick with such food as is suitable and best. At present there is at least one inmate suffering because this is not done. Subject to the qualification made by our answers above and these remarks, we consider the condition of the home good." One of the qualifications referred to: "Meat almost entirely of western bacon; sometimes fresh meat. All of this in sufficient quantity, but we consider the sameness of the diet and the character of meats bad for the inmates."

[23] *Ibid.*

Cleveland County. This county reports a new home, main building of brick with eighteen rooms and three wooden buildings of two rooms each. "One of the best in the State."

Columbus County. The attention of the county commissioners has been called to the fact that the keeper of the county home drinks. They promise to dismiss him at the end of the year.

Craven County. The buildings are old and so badly constructed that they must be cold in winter.

Guilford County. "We think our paupers are well fed with such provisions as are furnished, but we think that for old and infirm people, such as these, there should be a more palatable diet. They get wheat bread twice a week. We think they ought to have it every day if the Commissioners are able to furnish it, and with other things that they would relish."

Halifax County. "As chairman of the Board of County Commissioners of Halifax, I have charge of the Home, and am doing all in my power to make the inmates comfortable, and have made arrangements for them to have preaching oftener. They are well fed and clothed, and are now well cared for." This institution cared for forty-six inmates. The Superintendent was paid fifteen dollars per month. The chairman of the county board declared him to be a satisfactory officer. Diet for inmates consisted of two and a half pounds of meat, one peck of meal, sugar, coffee, flour, rice, fish, etc., weekly. One suspects that the first two were the most important in the list.

Harnett County. "Food: meat and bread as required, at a cost of $1.25 weekly." There were no physician, no land cultivated, no crops, no religious services.

Haywood County. Keeper paid two dollars per month per inmate. "Premises, a small country farm; the county owns none." Nine inmates. "Several of these should be properly cared for by their own kindred, as we think, but the county will not cavil over it at present. The county commissioners are all clever gentlemen, and disposed to do right."

Jackson County. Five log houses, two framed houses, "ventilation by plenty of cracks. . . . No inmates can be accommodated very comfortably by the present arrangements."

Montgomery County. "Five of the eleven in the Home ought to be out among relatives or friends, earning their own support."

New Hanover County. House of correction in connection with the county home.

Tyrrell County. "Since March 1st, 1891, the County Commissioners have not been able to procure any person to occupy the place as there were no inmates or applicants for admission.[24]

The calling of the attention of officials and the public to the problem of the poor, by the State Board of Charities, seems to have had some effect. In the report of the board for 1893 the secretary declares that "County Homes are better supplied with comforts; warmth, clothing and food of greater variety and better quality." And he continues: "Attention is respectfully called to reports through our Boards of new Homes built for the counties of Alamance, Beaufort, Macon, McDowell, Mecklenburg, Robeson, Sampson, and Swain; and of the very great improvement in buildings, appliances or management in the counties of Chatham, Davidson, Duplin, Durham, Halifax, Madison, Onslow, Person, New Hanover, Wake, and Watauga."[25]

But the secretary is not always so confident of progress. In 1894, after the caution that because of economic conditions and the force of custom, "it is too much to ex-

[24] *Ibid.,* pp. 42 ff.
[25] North Carolina State Board of Public Charities, *Biennial Report, 1893-95,* p. 8.

5. BETTER TYPES OF COUNTY HOMES BUILT TWO DECADES AGO

Wake County Hospital (County Home)

pect, to anticipate, that sanitary reforms in public institutions will at once be accepted, especially if involving any unusual outlay"; and that "public opinion must be carefully informed and wisely led, for it cannot be stemmed by attack, however enthusiastic," he says:

And yet, in view of the lamentable condition of certain jails and "homes" it doubtless is necessary that a salutary shock should be administered to neglectful officials, accustomed to satisfy themselves with the perfunctory report of grand juries, made after a visitation especially prepared for. Great credit should be given to those of our judges who have fearlessly required that the law should be complied with in the case of the unfortunate and even the criminal. Especially is honor due to the Hon. Spier Whitaker for the thorough investigation, at his instance, of the condition and management of many jails and homes.[26]

Again in the report for the years 1901-2 he writes:

But a lamentable condition of affairs yet exists in many counties as regards the condition and management of the Homes for the Aged and Infirm. Taken as a whole, it must be acknowledged that the provision for the honest poor does not equal that for the criminal although there is no jail that is too well cared for. The State institutions are the pride of its people, managed by officers of high qualifications, and in touch with the progress of the times. It is the forlorn poor houses, as they have been called which need the special and fostering oversight of intelligent men and women.[27]

He had already in an earlier part of the report called

[26] North Carolina State Board of Public Charities, *Report*, *1893-95*, pp. 127-28.
[27] North Carolina State Board of Public Charities, *Report*, *1901-02*, p. 181.

attention to the lack of uniformity when one county was compared with another:

It is not easy to see upon what basis the affairs of one county are managed without any system of relief other than the admission of three to five persons to a county home, while, in another, besides the home, monthly payments are made to more than a hundred persons.[28]

In the biennial report for 1897-1898, he points out that "we cannot be said to possess any system in our treatment" of the poor. One county may have a modern, well-equipped building;

another county may possess a Home which is a mere collection of log-huts, sometimes falling hovels, in distant places, out of sight and reach of the hand of ordinary charity; sometimes without a farm, or situated, it may be, upon the most barren spot to be purchased because of its cheapness; without stock to work it, or proper tools; in some cases without even a kitchen garden, surrounded by bushes and briars, with windows long without glass, leaking roofs, gaping walls, and only idleness and dirt within.

Still another county refuses altogether to provide a Home, and privately or publicly turns the care of the aged and infirm over to him who charges the least; possibly to the man whose conscience will permit him to afford less comfort at less cost than any other person can bring himself to, that a profit may still be afforded out of the scale of misery and want that human nature can endure and exist. To such refinement has the science of enforced privation reached that the poor were let at $2.12½ monthly last season in at least one county of our proud and chivalrous State, which yearly sends missionaries across the ocean to find the heathen.[29]

[28] *Loc. cit.*

[29] North Carolina State Board of Public Charities, *Report, 1897-98.*

The report stresses the importance of moving the county homes out of the remote corners; of securing fertile lands; of furnishing the farms with tools and stock; and of producing vegetables. The secretary suggests the advisability of maintaining a workhouse in connection with the county home, to which vagrants and other misdemeanants might be sentenced to work the farm, and the desirability of providing suitable occupation for the inmate poor. "The most important element in the Home," he says, "is the Superintendent. Yet he is carelessly chosen, very often for a few dollars of mistaken economy."[30]

The reports of the boards of visitors of the various counties extending over a quarter of a century from the reorganization of the State Board of Charities throw a flood of light upon the administration of poor relief in the state. There are here, of course, several standards for judging the excellence or lack of excellence in county homes. There were boards of visitors who were interested chiefly in making the best showing possible for their counties. To this group belonged the good old doctor in a county whose county home consisted of four small, cheap, framed cottages, let biennially to the lowest "responsible" bidder, as low as five dollars per month per inmate. During a period of several years, when the State Board of Charities was attempting to rate the county homes as "excellent," "good," "fair," "inferior,"

[30] North Carolina State Board of Public Charities, *Biennial Report, 1897-98*, p. 41.

and "bad," this home was reported "excellent."[31] Anyone who knew this institution would wonder by what sort of standard it could ever have been rated above "inferior."

In a second group were those visitors whose only conception of a county home was the sort of thing that existed in their own county, and who, having no means of comparison concluded that as county homes go their institution was about all that could be expected.

But there was also the intelligent observer who knew incompetency, dirt, and squalor when he saw them and who had the courage to point them out. To this class, evidently, belonged the visitor who in 1902 reported:

> The place is truly a "poor house." I am seventy years old and I never saw a place so utterly destitute of all means of comfort. The houses are old log structures; and the logs are rotten. The chimneys are built in the middle, or between the houses, and would have fallen but for the support of the logs. There is not a shade tree in one hundred yards, and it is one of the most horrid places I ever saw used for the purpose. It will be impossible to live comfortably in the house in winter.[32]

It is evident from the official reports of this period that not only was there no state-wide uniformity in the construction of almshouses or the administration of poor relief despite the efforts of the State Board of Public Charities, but there was rarely any well established and continuous standard in any individual county. Sometimes,

[31] North Carolina State Board of Public Charities, *Biennial Report, 1893-95*, p. 75, Watauga County.

[33] North Carolina State Board of Public Charities, *Biennial Report, 1901-02*, p. 67.

6. ALLEGHANY COUNTY HOME

This cheap cottage represents the provision made by Alleghany County for her indoor poor until a year ago, when provision was made for keeping the poor of this county in the county home of an adjoining county

because conditions in a particular home had become especially bad, or because the county happened to elect a board of county commissioners more than usually progressive, a new home was built or a higher type of superintendent employed, or such a superior superintendent was secured by mere accident, and for a period there existed really creditable conditions in that particular home. Then the home lost its newness, or the commissioners were changed, or a different superintendent took charge, and this home almost immediately became one of the intolerable places. The Iredell County Home is a good illustration. In 1849 Miss Dix proclaimed it a credit to any state.[33] This excellence, it was pointed out, must be attributed largely to the superiority of the superintendent and his wife. About 1890 this institution was again in the limelight, but for a different reason. The buildings were condemned by the board of county visitors as unfit and unsanitary and the management as poor;[34] the judge of the superior court visited the institution with the grand jury, and the county commissioners were indicted.[35] Some improvements seem to have been made, but in 1901 it was reported of the buildings that "three old log houses" were in a "dilapidated condition," that the land was poor, and that thirty inmates were housed in buildings with a capacity of twenty-five.[36] In 1913 there was

[33] See p. 60.
[34] North Carolina State Board of Public Charities, *Biennial Report, 1893-95*, p. 58.
[35] *Ibid.*, p. 10.
[36] North Carolina State Board of Public Charities, *Biennial Report, 1901-02*, p. 208.

another change in the status of this institution. A new plant, then perhaps the best in the state, was built and for some years the Iredell County Home was the show place of the kind in North Carolina. It is still well kept, and the farm is the finest county home farm in the state.

The last report of the Board of Charities before its reorganization in 1917 is interesting for purposes of comparison. There were no reports from twelve counties. Twenty-five of the counties then reporting had brick buildings. Fourteen had some sort of arrangement for fire protection. Fifteen plants were heated by steam and one other by furnace. Thirteen hundred and fifty inmates were reported. The cost of maintenance per month per inmate ranged from four to twelve and a half dollars. The average was six dollars and sixty-seven cents. The total cost of maintenance for county homes amounted to $108,246. Six counties had no county homes; and five of the existing homes were unoccupied. In addition to the poor in the county homes, 3,774 persons were given outdoor relief. For this purpose a total of $92,803 was spent.[37]

The period under consideration witnessed the assumption by the state of the care of special classes of the poor. In the period prior to the Civil War, covered by the preceding chapter, it had already entered the field of preventing pauperism, by providing for the education of the deaf and the blind. This policy was continued and

[37] North Carolina State Board of Public Charities, *Annual Report, 1916*, p. 77.

the attendance of these classes of children of both races
was made compulsory.[38]

The state had also, five years prior to the outbreak of
the Civil War, opened a hospital for the insane, but this
was maintained at the expense of the various counties.
The Constitution of 1868 made the care of the insane a
duty of the state, and it was accordingly written into
the law that

as the constitution declares that the general assembly
shall provide that all the deaf-mutes, the blind and the
insane of the State shall be cared for at the charge of
the State, the indebtedness of the counties for, and on
account of, the asylum shall be forgiven and discharged,
and hereafter no county shall levy any tax for the support of the insane asylum.[39]

Additional facilities were provided by the state
for the care of the insane by the opening in 1880 of a
hospital at Goldsboro for Negro insane and of a second
hospital for white insane, in 1883, at Morganton. The law
provided also that preference in admissions should
be given to the indigent,[40] a requirement not always met
in practice. In 1909 special provision was made for the
treatment of white epileptics at the Raleigh hospital.[41]
Negro epileptics may be admitted to the Goldsboro
hospital. These provisions have made practicable the
removal of most of the violently insane and a considerable number of epileptics from the county homes. These

[38] *Public Laws of North Carolina, 1907*, chap. 1007; *Extra Session, 1908*, chap. 141.
[39] *Public Laws of North Carolina, 1868-69*, chap. 67, sec. 28.
[40] *Public Laws of North Carolina, 1899*, chap. 1.
[41] *Public Laws of North Carolina, 1909*, chap. 910.

county institutions, as we have already seen, still attempt
to care for a considerable number of the mildly insane.

Toward the close of the period an additional step
was taken in state care of special classes in the establishment of an institution for the care of the white feeble-
minded. This institution, now known as Caswell Training
School, was founded in 1911.[42] With a capacity of four
hundred inmates, it is hopelessly inadequate to cope with
the problem of the care of the feeble-minded in the state.
It has, however, to some extent relieved the county homes
of the burden imposed by this class.

The latter part of the period also saw the beginning
of a state sanatorium for the treatment of tuberculosis.[43]
While the state did not at this time place the benefits of
this institution within reach of the poor, charitably inclined organizations and individuals from time to time
have made it possible for persons to go there who otherwise might have become charges upon the counties.

In 1891 the legislature made provision for a Confederate Soldiers' Home to which may be admitted

such deserving, needy Confederate Soldiers as shall have
served in any North Carolina command in the late war,
or who shall have served in the Confederate army and
shall be a bona fide citizen of the state.[44]

Prior to the establishment of this institution a number
of these old soldiers were found in the county homes.[45]

[42] *Public Laws of North Carolina, 1911,* chap. 87.
[43] *Public Laws of North Carolina, 1907,* chap. 964.
[44] *Public Laws of North Carolina, 1891,* chap. 60.
[45] North Carolina State Board of Public Charities, *Biennial Report, 1891-92.*

This provision for the state care of Confederate soldiers was supplemented in 1913 by the establishment at Fayetteville of the North Carolina Confederate Woman's Home for

deserving, needy and dependent wives and widows of North Carolina Confederate Soldiers and other worthy dependent women of the Confederacy who are bona fide residents of this State.[46]

Under the auspices mainly of the churches and fraternal orders, with only a minimum of aid from the state, there were organized within this period a score of orphanages. While these institutions have taken many children who otherwise would have been cared for in some way in families, their own or others, in some cases doubtless to the benefit of the child, they have also taken a considerable number who would have gone to the county home.

It was in the care of these special classes, which is not usually thought of as poor relief, that the half century covered by this chapter witnessed real progress. Within the limits usually recognized by county officials and by the public as the field of poor relief, there was no particular development or change in theory or in practice. The growth of the workhouse in connection with the county home, it is true, was checked, but only because the counties thought they had discovered a method of employing the labor of prisoners at a greater profit. The chain gang supplanted the workhouse. Only a few counties retained the workhouse alongside the almshouse.

[46] *Public Laws of North Carolina, 1913,* chap. 62.

The poorhouse continued, however, as a convenience to save judges the labor of thinking about the solution of certain types of difficult cases. Prisoners were occasionally sentenced to the county home with little regard to the facilities for handling them there. The county home continued the dumping ground for the wrecks of every type.[47]

A state board of charities had been created and charged with the supervision of almshouses, but this board was never given support to enable it to function efficiently and for nearly twenty years ceased to exist. It had, however, in the first few years of its existence and again after its reorganization courageously called attention to conditions. The first secretary of the later period of the board's existence, Captain C. B. Denson, was successful to some extent in arousing local interest in the county poorhouses by the appointment of visiting committees in the various counties. Upon his death Captain Denson was succeeded by his daughter, Miss Daisy Denson, the first woman to hold an important official position in North Carolina. These two officials succeeded,

[47] This interesting survival of the county home as a combination almshouse and institution for the punishment of misdemeanants perhaps deserves more extended notice. Not only do certain counties, like Durham and New Hanover, have workhouses alongside the county home, but others, like Guilford, Durham, and Alamance, have made provision for quartering women prisoners within the home itself. The custom of sentencing women to any county home is recognized by law in the provision that deductions from sentence allowed for good behavior "shall apply also to women sentenced to a county farm or county home" (*Consolidated Statutes of North Carolina, 1360*). Throughout the period under consideration young boys also were frequently sentenced by the courts to the county home.

almost without funds, in gathering a considerable amount of information, in keeping themselves surprisingly well informed as to conditions in the counties, and in correcting from time to time some of the worst conditions in various localities. The system of poor relief as a whole, however, responded very slowly to the efforts of the Board of Public Charities.

CHAPTER V

PRESENT STATUS OF COUNTY HOMES AND THEIR ADMINISTRATION

In 1917 the State Board of Public Charities was reorganized as the State Board of Charities and Public Welfare; the number of its members was increased; its powers and duties were enlarged; and provision was made for the replacement of the Secretary by a Commissioner of Public Welfare and a staff of trained workers. The law of 1917, amended and strengthened in 1919, made provision also for the organization of the state on a county-unit basis, with a local board and a superintendent of public welfare in each county.

The new board was specifically charged with the supervision of charitable institutions. One of the first acts of the new commissioner, therefore, was to secure a survey of the county home situation. Upon invitation the National Committee for Mental Hygiene came to the state to study the state hospitals for the insane and county homes with special reference to the mentally diseased found in these institutions. This study involved fifty-six county homes. Somewhat unfortunately the visitors to the county homes were divided into two groups, each visiting a separate group of county homes. At the head of one group was the representative of the visiting organization. At the head of the other was an official of a local state institution. The visitor from without the state had a keen eye for the defects of the institutions visited and was in-

7. LIVING ROOM, CHATHAM COUNTY HOME

The Chatham County home has two comfortable living rooms for its inmates—one for whites and one for Negroes—that are actually used. The fire was not built in order to have a picture made. The visitors who made it dropped in unannounced on an autumn day when it was barely cool enough for a fire to be comfortable. Two inmates are shown as they were dressed when the visitors arrived.

clined to play up these shortcomings in a sensational manner. The visitor from within the state, on the other hand, was inclined to make the most of the good points found and occasionally to overlook rather serious defects. In one instance, for example, he pronounced "modern" a county home building which is so poorly arranged that the bath rooms for the inmates can be reached from their rooms only by going out on a porch. But in spite of the extreme and opposite points of view of the investigators, the report submitted to the State Board of Charities and Public Welfare in 1920 is a very valuable document. Not the least valuable feature is the collection of photographs of the county homes visited.

This survey marked the beginning of a period of activity in building new county homes. In at least one case the building of a new plant was apparently the direct outcome of the survey. The criticisms of conditions in the Guilford County Home were severe and quite sensationally presented. "The report," says the State Board of Charities and Public Welfare, "caused a storm of protest; but with her characteristic progressive spirit, Guilford County replied to the criticisms by erecting an up-to-date county home plant at a cost of one hundred and twenty thousand dollars"[1]

Continuing its study of poor relief in the counties, the State Board of Charities and Public Welfare in 1922 made a more exhaustive survey of the system throughout

[1] *Poor Relief in North Carolina*, North Carolina State Board of Charities and Public Welfare, Special Bulletin No. 4, 1925. In the preparation of this chapter free use has been made of this bulletin, which was written by the author while a member of the staff of the State Board of Charities and Public Welfare.

the state. The information thus gathered and subsequent
data secured in the course of the routine duties of the
board were published in a special bulletin on poor relief
early in 1925,[2] and in the biennial reports of the board
for the years 1920-22, 1922-24, and 1924-26. These reports present a rather complete picture of poor relief and
especially of the county home of the present day.

County homes in North Carolina still include every
type and condition of building from wretched shacks and
log cabins to creditable and even elaborate and expensive
plants. The Wake County Hospital, as the county home
is locally called, is one of the most imposing looking
buildings in the vicinity of the state capitol. The Guilford
County Home is one of the most conspicious buildings or
group of buildings in the neighborhood of Greensboro.
The county homes of Buncombe, Durham, Nash, and
Robeson are in the same class, while a score of others
fall only slightly below these. Forty-four counties
have buildings alone valued at $15,000 or more. Twenty-
five counties have buildings worth $40,000 or more.
Several have cost from $100,000 to $175,000 each. Between 1919 and 1926 twenty-seven counties[3] built new
homes. At the close of the period one county was building and another had its plans approved.[4] More than a

[2] *Ibid.*

[3] These counties are: Alamance, Burke, Caldwell, Caswell, Chatham, Cherokee, Clay, Durham, Franklin, Guilford, Halifax, Harnett, Jackson, Johnston, Martin, Nash, Northampton, Onslow,
Person, Polk, Randolph, Robeson, Rowan, Rutherford, Sampson,
Stanly, Vance, Watauga, Wayne, and Wilson.

[4] North Carolina State Board of Charities and Public Welfare,
Biennial Report, 1924-26, p. 31.

8. THE GUILFORD COUNTY HOME

million dollars have been expended on new county homes in the state within this period of eight years.

An interesting point in connection with the building of new county homes is the number that have been re-located—brought out from the back country to the main highways near the county seats. There are still twenty-one homes, however, that are not on a public highway. In 1923 the road leading to one of these was impassable in dry weather for a Ford car.

The evidence of progress presented by the existence of these buildings is somewhat deceptive. Measured in terms of money invested or in terms of equipment as expressed in buildings, progress has been made. Judged by any other standard there has been improvement. But in too many cases the progress has been more apparent than real. Some of the better buildings have been poorly planned. The number that show evidences of having been planned by one who had some conception of the problems presented by the county home is increasing, but there are still too many of the other class. There is often inadequate provision for the segregation of the sexes. In the newer homes, infirmary wards have usually been provided for the sick; but these wards are usually either inadequately furnished or not furnished at all. Quite frequently they are not used or are used as other rooms for the ordinary housing of inmates. There are exceptions, of course. The new Rowan County Home, for instance, has a well-equipped hospital ward, and the Vance County Hospital has a department for the care of the aged and infirm poor, the emphasis in this case being on the hospital functions of the institution.

From the point of view of modern conveniences there is still much to be desired. Of eighty-five of the ninety county homes then in operation that reported on the matter of lighting in 1922, forty still used kerosene lamps; five, lanterns; and one, candles. This number has been somewhat reduced, doubtless, by the building of modern plants in a few of the counties; but there are still about forty using these out-of-date methods of lighting. A reason for backwardness in this respect is not hard to find. Many county commissioners living in the country do not have electric lights. Certainly the average citizen does not have this convenience. Commissioner, grand juror, and taxpayer alike, therefore, naturally conclude that there is no good reason for taxing the people to provide these luxuries for the poor. He forgets that with the scant supervision usually provided at the county home, the kerosene lamp endangers not only the property of the county but the lives of the inmates. In the summer of 1924 the building for colored inmates at the Lenoir County Home was burned at night and with it the only occupant. It is surmised that this inmate, a feeble old woman, who was in the building alone, attempted to light her lamp and accidentally set fire to the building.

A large number of the homes, including some of those with substantial buildings, are poorly furnished. Often the furnishings are of the crudest sort. A cheap bed— usually a double bed—a cheap straight chair for each inmate, sometimes a table—these are the typical furnishings of a room in the majority of our county homes. Such luxuries as closets, bureaus, chests, or mirrors in the inmates' rooms are the exception rather than the rule.

9. ROBESON COUNTY HOME

About twenty-five of the county homes in the state report complete modern conveniences for all inmates—hot and cold running water, adequate bathing facilities, steam heat, electric lights, and sewerage, including separate toilets for the different races and sexes.

Considered somewhat more in detail from the point of view of adequate conveniences, there were in 1922 twenty-four institutions reporting steam heat; forty-five, stoves, and the remainder, open fireplaces. Of eighty-seven counties reporting on the presence or absence of bathtubs, thirty-four had one or more; fifty-three had none; twenty-nine used galvanized wash tubs; six had no facilities. This statement must be modified by the evidence that some of the county homes having bathtubs do not use them for the purpose of bathing. In one small new county home a representative of the State Board of Charities and Public Welfare found each of the two bathtubs partially filled with straw to give the hens a place to nest. He does not believe that the hens were often disturbed in order to give the inmates a chance to take a bath. In another county the superintendent, in reply to a question as to the frequency of baths, said: "Don't take 'em. Make 'em clean up about every two weeks—change clothes and bed." In a third home, it is reported, the inmates refuse to make use of the bathtubs, preferring "local applications." It is not surprising, therefore, that of the eighty-one counties reporting on this item, only about one-half—forty-three—say that the inmates are clean of person and dress. Only twenty-one out of seventy-nine reporting had one or more living rooms for the use of the inmates. Thirty-five out of seventy-five did not have window space sufficient to give the amount of light desirable in the rooms used by inmates. Thirty-four counties four years ago reported modern sewerage systems. Eighteen others had sanitary privies. Thirty had open closets. Three reported "no facilities."

The source of water supply was reported as follows: open wells, twenty-nine; springs, eighteen; pumps, fourteen; deep wells, twenty; mains from city systems, four. A total of forty-seven counties used either open wells or else springs which are almost equally dangerous for institutional use. One county home superintendent in a county in the northeastern section of the state told the writer proudly that he had fine water—he had never seen any "wiggle-tails" in it.

In regard to each of these items half a dozen county homes have moved up into the modern class since 1922.

The kitchen and dining-room of the average county home are the least attractive places about it. They are poorly furnished and often inadequately screened. There are several county homes in the state, of course, which are exceptions to this. Usually the superintendent's wife has been accustomed to only the most primitive mode of living and is helpless when confronted with the problems of an institution. Frequently dirty and diseased inmates help with the work in the kitchen and dining-room. In one county home in the state a filthy-looking, old insane woman continually potters about the flour bin. Few county home kitchens or dining rooms are free from flies. Often these are present in swarms.

In other parts of the "home" also there is often lack of cleanliness. Not infrequently the chief effort in this direction takes the form of a liberal use of disinfectant as a substitute for soap and water. There are perhaps two reasons for this. To go about squirting vile-smelling stuff out of a "gun" appeals strongly to many county home superintendents, as it does also to the average jailer. It is a poor substitute for soap and water; but it is more easily applied, and it is not yet so definitely associated in the minds of these officials with labor. Then, in the second place, some of the manufacturers of disinfectants offer very liberal premiums, graduated to fit the size of the order. The Chemo Company of Buffalo, New York, for example, at least as late as April 1, 1926, was offering as premiums for orders of disinfectants a twenty-six piece set of Rogers silverware; electric floor lamps; sewing machines; talking machines; Elgin gold watches; New Haven mahogany eight-day clocks; rocking chairs; rugs; refrigerators, white enamel interior, up to one hundred pounds ice capacity; electric vacuum cleaners; Savage hammerless repeating rifles; trunks; traveling bags; bicycles; etc., etc. Any qualms of conscience that the county home superintendent might have are allayed by the statement that "we charge no more for our goods than before we gave premiums." Then there need be no embarrassment about the articles' arriving together, for it is stated "if you prefer, we will send premiums at once and ship goods any time within the next three months."

With county home keepers thus encouraged in seeking substitutes for cleanliness it is not particularly surprising that twenty-eight homes report the presence of bedbugs. Recently when a progressive board of county commissioners in one of the largest counties of the state decided to renovate the county home, a painter employed on the job reported that occasionally when he started to paint over a particularly dark spot on the wall, the dark spot began immediately to scatter in all directions.

On a slight eminence overlooking a beautiful river valley, with mountains in the background, stands an attractive brick building that cost several tens of thousands of dollars, the county home in one of the best of the mountain counties. "You will want a picture of this for your bulletin," said one of two members of the staff of the State Commissioner of Public Welfare as he and his colleague stopped in front of the institution one afternoon in September, 1924. They entered. He may still think a picture should have appeared in the bulletin, but for a somewhat different reason. There was little evidence of intelligent care anywhere within, but the climax was reached in a room whose walls were covered with finger prints—hundreds and hundreds of them. "What caused these?" asked the visitor. "That's where he's killed chinches," replied the son of the superintendent, indicating by a nod of the head the old man who occupied the room.

Practically all the county homes in the state have considerable farms, or at least areas of land, attached. As shown by a careful census made in 1922 of the ninety-four counties owning poor farms, only six counties—Beaufort, Carteret, Dare, Hyde, Pasquotank, and Tyrrell—had holdings of less than twenty-five acres. Eight others—Craven, Lenoir, Madison, Moore, Richmond, Robeson, Wilson, and Yancey—reported acreages ranging from twenty-five to fifty. Twenty-nine counties had

10. "On a Slight Eminence Overlooking a Beautiful River Valley"

farms of from one hundred to two hundred acres; twenty counties, of from two hundred to four hundred acres; and nine, of more than four hundred acres. Within the last four years Alamance, Chatham, Vance, Nash, and Halifax have built new homes on reduced acreages. Randolph County has recently leased a part of its county home farm to the state to be used as a game preserve.[5]

As a rule the county home farms are poorly equipped with farm machinery and livestock. It is hardly necessary to add that they are poorly farmed. Thirty-six county homes, with farms ranging from a few acres to three hundred acres, in 1922 reported no farm machinery. The same number reported no livestock belonging to the county. It is most unusual to find any livestock except hogs—in some instances a fine herd—and an occasional cow. The keeper of the home who operates the farm usually furnishes his own machinery and stock. His financial condition is, almost without exception, such that he cannot furnish the equipment necessary for the efficient cultivation of the land entrusted to him. He therefore proceeds to work a portion of the land after the inefficient and, to the land itself as well as to the farmer, ruinous methods of the unsupervised tenant farmer. Only occasionally do we find a farm that shows evidence of intelligent management. Such an exception is the county home farm in Iredell County. Here, under the direction of an intelligent superintendent who has been in charge for twenty years, the county home farm has been brought to a state of productiveness scarcely surpassed in this excellent agricultural county.

[5] *Greensboro Daily News*, Dec. 11, 1927.

County homes in the state own approximately sixteen thousand acres of land. Of this about one-fourth, or a little more than four thousand acres, is in cultivation. Twelve thousand acres—three-fourths of the total acreage —are idle. Of this waste land, the keepers of the county homes report that five thousand additional acres are cultivable.

A few specific instances may give a clearer picture of the actual conditions on county home farms. Among the counties which in 1922 owned no farm machinery or live- stock in connection with the county home farm are Ashe, with farm lands reported to be worth thirteen thousand dollars; Cleveland, with a farm valued at thirty-two thousand five hundred dollars; and Johnston, with lands worth twenty-four thousand dollars. Anson, with hold- ings in lands for the county home valued at sixteen thousand dollars, owned no farm machinery and had thirty-five dollars invested in livestock. Guilford reported land worth thirty thousand dollars. She reported only two hundred dollars worth of farm machinery and no livestock. Now let us see how these farms are equipped by the various superintendents of the homes. Ashe County's farm of one hundred and forty acres was equip- ped by the superintendent. He owned two horses, five milch cows, three hogs, and thirty-five hens. There was no report as to the machinery which he owned for working the farm. The Anson County Home farm of two hundred and fourteen acres was equipped jointly by the county and the superintendent of the home. The superintendent owned two mules, one cow, three hogs, and forty hens. The county furnished one cow valued at thirty-five dollars. No farm machinery was reported. Whatever was used was owned by the superintendent. Johnston County's county home farm contained two hundred and forty acres, only fifty acres of which were in cultivation. "This land," said County Superintendent of Public Welfare H. V. Rose, "will produce a bale of cotton to the acre, or twelve hundred pounds of bright leaf tobacco." The livestock and farm machinery on this valuable farm were owned by the superintendent. At the time of the survey there were two mules, one horse, ten hogs, and forty hens. The report reads, "No cow at present." There had been none for a year, or at least no milk had been produced.

Seven county homes in 1922 had each two hundred or more idle acres. These are: Surry, with four hundred and twenty-five idle acres; Halifax, three hundred and forty acres; New Hanover, three hundred acres; Rutherford, three hundred acres; Nash, two hundred and fifty-two acres; Orange, two hundred and fifty acres; and Rockingham, two hundred acres. Taking the average value per acre assigned in the reports from these counties, we have represented by these two thousand two hundred and sixty-seven idle acres a total unproductive capital of one hundred and forty thousand dollars. Since that time Halifax and Nash have each completed new county homes on new and smaller farms. A number of other counties had as large a percentage of uncultivated land, bringing the total to twelve thousand acres.

It is evident, even from the incomplete figures available, that farming in connection with county homes in North Carolina is not generally profitable. But it would be a matter of little importance whether a county home farm pays, if it could be shown that the farm is producing in as great abundance as needed those foods which are best suited to the needs of the inmates and which may best be had in desirable quantity and quality only when produced at home. But this is rarely if ever true. Very rarely is there an intelligent effort to have a bountiful supply of vegetables for as nearly all of the year as is possible in that particular locality. As a rule the raising of vegetables is secondary to the production of a money crop. Recently, on a county home farm in the finest trucking section of the state, a representative of the State Board of Charities and Public Welfare found no early vegetables and no adequate provision for a later supply. While trainloads of early vegetables were being shipped from the immediate neighborhood, the only vegetable on hand for use in the institution was some spinach given by one of the county commissioners. Preparations were being made for a crop of corn. More often, as has already been said, the farming is done in such a slipshod way that neither vegetables nor other crops are a success. Usually the superintendent of the county home reports that he produces plenty of vegetables, but in most cases a look at the county home garden is proof that he does not appreciate the meaning of that expression. What is true of vegetables is also true of milk, eggs, and meats. An adequate supply of milk and butter is as unusual as an adequate supply of vegetables. Very few counties make any provision for a milk supply. This applies also to eggs. Practically the only kind of meat produced on the county home farm is hog meat. A few of the homes produce a considerable supply of this.

Supervision in the county homes in North Carolina is of a lower type even than the equipment. It has not yet become the general custom to pay salaries that will attract the type of men needed for the difficult task of operating a county home. Thirty-seven counties in 1924 paid their superintendent of the county home less than one hundred dollars cash per month. Nineteen paid six hundred dollars or less per year. Twenty counties still sold the keeping of the county home to the lowest bidder. The same number paid a stated amount per month per inmate.

The last biennial report of the State Board of Charities and Public Welfare says:

Most of the counties of the State have not secured the better qualified persons for county home superintendents, because the salaries paid are too low to attract the type of persons needed. Thirty-one counties out of sixty-four [reporting] pay their superintendents in actual money less than one hundred dollars per month. One county pays two hundred dollars per month for the services of the superintendent and his wife. Ten counties pay less than six hundred dollars per year.[6]

In addition to his salary, it should be borne in mind, however, the superintendent gets a house to live in and, usually, board for himself and family. In the eighty-three counties reporting in 1922 on this item the average age of the superintendent was forty-seven years. In many cases there were large families of children. These

[6] North Carolina State Board of Charities and Public Welfare, *Biennial Report, 1924-26,* p. 31.

were usually supported by the county. In one instance the county was supporting seventeen members of the superintendent's family in addition to paying eighteen dollars per month per inmate for sixteen inmates. He had a house and a hundred acres of cultivable land free of rent. In another county a new superintendent of the county home was recently elected. The retiring superintendent had ten children. He received house rent and food for his family in addition to his salary of seventy-five dollars a month. A cook was paid twenty dollars a month. Under such conditions seventy-five dollars a month is not a salary to be despised.

In twenty counties there were paid matrons. One county in 1922 paid its county home matron nine hundred dollars a year; three paid six hundred dollars; two paid two hundred and forty; the others paid less than four hundred dollars. More often the wife of the superintendent serves as matron without pay in her own name. Not infrequently she does the cooking, looks after the inmates and the house work, and cares for several small children of her own. This may be the chief reason for the type of superintendent most common in the state.

Whatever the reason, it is not unusual to find a superintendent who belongs to a class only slightly superior to most of the inmates. He is rarely to be compared with the other officials of the county. He is not the type of man who could be elected register of deeds or clerk of the court. His wife, of course, usually belongs to the same class as he. There are a few exceptions, but they are exceptions. Two instances in counties in widely separated sections of the state illustrate the type of superintendent and matron that is quite frequently found. In a county in which the tumble-down shacks called the county home are a disgrace, the single inmate, an old half-crazy negro man, was telling the visitor about the fat meat he had to eat. The keeper flew into a rage and hotly protested that he did not buy fat meat but "good shoulder meat." Two years later the same man was able to name two of the three county commissioners of his county, but when asked who was the register of deeds replied, "You're too hard for me."[7]

The following paragraphs from the biennial report of the State Board of Charities and Public Welfare for the years 1920-22 (pages 56-61) throw additional light on the type of management that has been common in county homes in recent years:

Two representatives of the State Board of Charities and Public Welfare were visting another county home. The superintendent was away. His wife was working in the cotton field. After a while she came in. She was barefooted. Her baby was nursing as she walked along, and her dress was thrown open from the neck to the waist. Her mother, her mother's sister, and her father's brother were inmates of the home. She was matron without salary.

About three years ago a feeble-minded youth of nineteen, and a feeble-minded woman of seventy, inmates of the Forsyth County Home, strayed down to the office of the register of deeds, procured a marriage license, looked up a Methodist preacher, were married, went—presumably on foot—for a short bridal tour, and then returned to the county home, where they have been living happily ever since. Luckily they were not both nineteen.

In Davidson County a man was sentenced to the county

7 North Carolina State Board of Charities and Public Welfare, *Biennial Report, 1922-24*, p. 76.

chain-gang. He proved to be so feeble-minded that he could not be used on the roads, so he was transferred for the remainder of his sentence to the county home. There he formed an attachment for a feeble-minded woman thirty years old, herself born in the county home. A child was born as the result. Fortunately it died.

In Watauga County a few years ago, near Blowing Rock, an old feeble-minded man and a feeble-minded girl were found living together without the formality of a marriage ceremony. The good people of the community arose in indignation and sent the offenders to jail. A few weeks later they came up for trial before the Superior Court. The judge threw up his hands and said, "I don't know what to do with this case." Some one suggested that they be allowed to get married. A lawyer passed the hat and collected the money to buy the license. A justice of the peace was called from the crowd in the courtroom. The pair were married. Within the next few years three children were born. The old man died. The woman and two of her children were taken to the county home. She has since given birth to two other children in the county home, and she is still a young woman. She has a mental age of about six years.[8]

[8] In 1926 another chapter was added to this story of the lack of intelligent control of this feeble-minded woman. On the pretext that she was to be married to an old man she was allowed to leave the County Home. She returned to the same general neighborhood in which she had first attempted some sort of family life. This time she "settled" just over the line in Caldwell County. The old man according to previous arrangement was her partner in this venture. Again, as it later developed, there had been no marriage ceremony. The pair was joined by another feeble-minded young woman, a cousin of the first, who also had been for some time previously an inmate of the Watauga County Home. After some months the two women tired of the old man and drove him away. At about the same time that the dissolution of this partnership became known, it was reported that the cousin was soon to give birth to a child.

In mitigation of the crime that Watauga County has com-

A generation ago there came to the Nash County Home a woman and her daughter, a young girl. This feeble-minded girl grew up in the county home. She is now an old woman. She has given birth in the county home to ten children, one of whom is colored. Some time—at the suggestion of the superintendent of the home, one version of the story goes—she married a misshapen, feeble-minded inmate of the institution. He thinks he is the father of two of her ten children. Two of the ten died in infancy. Six were placed. Two are in the county home. One of these, a young woman about twenty-four years old, is the mother of four children, including twins only a few months old. In fairness to the county home, it should be stated that she was out of that institution for a few weeks about the time of the conception of the twins.

Forty years ago a girl in Montgomery County was so paralyzed at the birth of her first illegitimate child that she never walked since. Soon after the occurrence she was taken to the county home. Ten years later she gave birth to a second child by a man who lived near the county home. She has since married successively two inmates of the county home. Both are dead. The father of her second child has for a number of years been an inmate of the home. Six years ago he married a feeble-minded woman thirty-five years old, also an inmate of the home.

The following story was told a few weeks ago by the keeper of the Scotland County home. Within the last year there was among the inmates of the home a Negro man forty-five years old, who was being treated by the county physician for syphilis. He began paying attention to a negro woman, also an inmate. The keeper heard it rumored that they were to marry. He did not discourage it, as the man seemed to be getting better, and the

mitted against society in the mishandling of these two women, it should be noted that two unsuccessful attempts were made to secure the admission of the first of these women to Caswell Training School—the first by a socially-minded citizen and the second by the county superintendent of public welfare, or rather by his wife, who is unofficially his assistant.

keeper thought he might make a good tenant on the farm. Illicit sex relations between the couple were discovered. The man left, but returned in a few days, when he was told by the keeper that he must leave, and that the woman must also go as soon as she was able. The man left, but returned in a day or so with a buggy and took the woman.

Durham County maintains a combination county home and workhouse. Both men and women are sent to the workhouse. A few months ago a low-grade feeble-minded white girl, an inmate of the county home proper, gave birth to a child, evidently of negro parentage. The only explanation is the presence of negro prisoners.

In Burke County a few months ago an imbecile negro girl, who was herself born in the county home, gave birth to a child by a white father.

Some of these, of course, are striking cases of their type, but the type is by no means rare in county homes in North Carolina. In fact as one goes into the history of the various county homes for a few years back, it seems that the county home is fortunate that has not had its scandal in connection with a feeble-minded inmate.

The 1922 survey tried to secure some information as to the education of superintendents. Eighty counties gave some sort of information on this subject. In seventy-four of these the superintendent had less than a high school education. Six superintendents are recorded as having a high school education or more. Since then the only superintendent who had any college training has been removed because he did not belong to the same political faction as the county commissioners. A large number of these superintendents are practically illiterate. A few cannot read and write. Most of the superintendents were farmers before they came to the county homes—sixty-nine out of eighty about whom information on this item was obtained. Thirty of these were tenant farmers. The eleven who were not farmers came from various occupations— merchant, salesman, carpenter, mason, jailer, policeman, "moonshiner."

Until recently there has been little supervision over the superintendent. The county commissioners, who, since the Civil War, have had the general oversight of poor relief, have usually contented themselves with employing a superintendent every two years. Sometimes he is chosen because he is the cheapest man; sometimes because he has been of service to the political faction in power. Sometimes the commissioners are genuinely interested; but they are usually busy men giving one or two days a month to the affairs of the county. In any case, the county home as a rule gets little supervision from this source. Occasionally, however, a board of county commissioners or some member of the board gives thought and intelligent supervision to the institution; or, occasionally a good man or woman or a man with a good wife is employed, and things go well at the county home with a minimum of supervision.

Since 1919 the law has provided that the county superintendent of public welfare shall "have, under the control of the county commissioners, the care and supervision of the poor, and administer the poor funds." This law seems to have been variously interpreted by various boards of county commissioners. A few boards, even in counties that have full-time superintendents of public welfare, are apparently ignorant of the existence of the law. In a large number of counties, however, all new applications for admission to the county home are re-

ferred to the superintendent of public welfare for investigation and recommendation. The number of counties
in this group is constantly increasing.

In several counties the results of giving the superintendent of public welfare a free hand have been quite notable.
Vance County is an interesting example. Here the county
owned some wooden buildings situated on a farm a few
miles from the county seat. The institution was poorly
kept. In 1921 a new superintendent of public welfare
was elected. She took stock of the welfare problems of
the county. One of the immediate needs was to find some
way to care for the inmates of the county, home. The
county commissioners agreed that something must be
done. A smaller piece of land near the county seat was
selected and an attractive but inexpensive building of
brick was planned and built. It was attractively furnished
under the supervision of the superintendent of public welfare. During the months while the new home was under
construction she was skillfully preparing the inmates for
the change. They were led to look forward to moving into
the new home as an event of their lives. Finally the day
came. Each inmate was moved to his or her own small
room, or in the case of one or two old couples into a suite
of two small rooms. One old Negro man, who, according
to his own account, was "goin' on more than a hundred"
years old, had his first experience with a bathtub and
enjoyed it so much that he did not want to get out. A low-
grade, feeble-minded Negro woman, whose room at the
old home had always been filthy as a pig pen, was given
instruction in caring for her new room (for in this new
type of county home, where each inmate has his own

room, he is led to feel a responsibility for that room and to take pride in keeping it in order). This woman has rarely forgotten to make her bed, clean up her room, and raise her windows before leaving the room in the morning. The writer visited this home without warning at eight o'clock in the morning. The inmates were just finishing breakfast. With the exception of one room, occupied by a very old inmate who had remained late in bed, the beds were already made and the rooms in order, this work having been done, practically without supervision, by the inmates. Every inmate was eager that his or her room should be seen. One Negro man, partially paralyzed, stood in his door pathetically anxious lest his room be overlooked.

The old county home, without any of the modern conveniences, cost the county for maintenance, in addition to any products of the farm used in the institution, five thousand dollars a year. The cost of maintenance for the first year in the new home, with its individual rooms, its attractive living rooms (one for each race) its commodious kitchen and dining rooms, with all modern conveniences, was one thousand eight hundred sixty dollars. The per capita cost in the old home was $28.89 per month; in the new home it was $10.41.[9]

But the original idea of the superintendent of public welfare had been that this was to be primarily a hospital. Toward making it such she now directed her energies. The results of these efforts are told in the report of the State Board of Charities and Public Welfare:

[9] North Carolina State Board of Charities and Public Welfare, *Biennial Report, 1922-24,* p. 75.

The regular population of the home has been reduced from twenty-five to seven. This has been accomplished by placing many of the applicants for admission to the county home in the home of some relative or neighbor and paying small sums for support. This is a sort of outdoor relief which may prove successful under proper supervision. It is usually cheaper and the individuals concerned are in many cases much happier. As Mrs. W. B. Waddill, Superintendent of Public Welfare for Vance County, has said, "Many paupers are the derelicts, the incapable, or the incapacitated, and very little can be done for them except to make them comfortable and happy, for this class of society possesses practically no constructive possibility." It is through the use of this plan that half of the county home has been converted into a hospital with a well-equipped operating room. A trained nurse is superintendent of the hospital home.[10]

The hospital has been approved as such by the Duke Foundation and the first year's appropriation, $2,410, from that fund toward its maintenance has just been received. The institution has now (June, 1927) only five in the department for the aged and infirm, who are not classified as hospital patients eligible for support from the Duke Foundation.

There are approximately eighteen hundred people in county homes in North Carolina.[11] In the matter of race the Negroes furnished somewhat more than their proportion of the inmates. In 1920, 29 per cent of the population of the state were Negroes. In 1922, 37 per cent of the inmates of the county homes

[10] North Carolina State Board of Charities and Public Welfare, *Biennial Report, 1924-26,* p. 31.

[11] *Loc. cit.*

were Negroes. Of the children under sixteen, it may be interesting to note, only 17 per cent were Negroes. The inmates are distributed among ninety-two county homes.
Eight counties do not maintain almshouses. The number
of inmates in the individual county homes varies from
one to one hundred and fifty. Twenty-six county homes in
1924 had fewer than ten inmates.[12] Eighteen out of
sixty-four reporting on this item in 1926 had fewer than
ten.[13] Seventy-one "homes" in 1924 had each fewer than
twenty-five inmates. Nine had forty or more. Only one
had more than one hundred.

In the 1922 survey the State Board of Charities and
Public Welfare made an effort to arrive at the actual
cost of maintaining paupers in the several county homes
in the state. The study showed monthly costs per capita
ranging from two dollars and a half to ninety dollars.
Similar figures, but taking into consideration only the
amounts paid from the county treasuries and not including farm products used in the homes, were compiled for
1923 and 1924. In this connection the *Biennial Report for
1922-24* says:

In estimating the per capita cost no account has been
taken of depreciation of buildings or of excess of interest on investment over products of the farm. If these
are added, the per capita cost in many instances will be
appreciably increased. Excluding these, the costs in many
counties are too high. Twenty-five dollars per month is
a big price to pay for the sort of care the inmates of

[12] North Carolina State Board of Charities and Public Welfare,
Biennial Report, 1922-24, p. 76.
[13] North Carolina State Board of Charities and Public Welfare,
Biennial Report, 1924-26, p. 31.

even the better county homes are getting. Yet the per capita cost per month in forty-eight county homes in 1921 was more than twenty-five dollars per month. Nine cost between thirty and forty dollars; eleven, between forty and fifty dollars; and five, over fifty dollars. The highest cost was $87.51 per capita per month.

In 1923, exclusive of farm and garden products used in the homes, the per capita cost per month in twenty-two county homes was twenty-five dollars a month or more. Four cost between thirty and forty dollars; two, between forty and fifty dollars; and five over fifty dollars. These were Columbus, with a monthly per capita cost of $50.08; Duplin, $55.56; Harnett, $64.34; Pitt, $95.11; and Brunswick, $103.73. Columbus reported an average of nine inmates; Duplin, six inmates; Harnett, three inmates; Pitt, ten inmates; and Brunswick, one inmate. For a part of the time Brunswick had none; so it is presumed that for part of the time she had two. Columbus has a farm of one hundred and twenty acres, valued exclusive of buildings at $10,000. Duplin has seventy acres, valued at $5,000. Harnett has sixty acres, worth $5,000. Pitt has one hundred and eighty acres, valued at $35,000. And Brunswick had one hundred acres, worth $5,000. In all cases these are values placed on these farms in 1922 by county officials.[14]

Reports in the files of the State Board of Charities and Public Welfare from forty counties for 1927 show an average per capita cost of $26.48 a month. The highest cost was in Halifax County, $57.82; the lowest in Columbus County, $5.74. Surry and Watauga counties were close seconds for lowest place with monthly per capita costs of $6.35 and $8.00 respectively. Pitt County had reduced costs to $22.09. Brunswick was paying $41.66 a month for caring for five inmates in her county home.

[14] North Carolina State Board of Charities and Public Welfare, *Biennial Report, 1922-24*, p. 79.

Other counties reporting costs of more than $40.00 per capita a month were Forsyth and Jackson.

The reports to the State Board of Charities and to the reorganized State Board of Charities and Public Welfare, which are fairly continuous since 1891, show that there has been but little increase in the number of inmates in county homes within thirty years. The actual numbers have increased since 1891 in twenty-six counties. In fifty-three counties there has been a decrease in actual numbers for the period of thirty-two years. In ten other counties there has been a decrease for several years. Considered in relation to the whole population of the various counties, the figures are still more interesting. Of the twenty-six counties in which there were increases in the numbers of inmates only thirteen show an increase per thousand population. And in two of these thirteen the ratio has shown a decrease within the last twenty years.

The general decrease in the ratio of indoor poor is due largely to the elimination of certain classes of persons who were formerly sent to the poorhouse in large numbers, or to progress toward such elimination. Children were formerly found in county homes in rather large numbers. The development of orphanages and of the North Carolina Children's Home Society has taken some of the children. The hospitals for the insane are caring for a large part of the insane. Caswell Training School has relieved the counties of the care of some of the feeble-minded. In many of the counties social investigation is taking the place of political expediency or lack of supervision in the admission of inmates.

In the survey of 1922, superintendents of public welfare reported six hundred and sixty-three cases of feeble-mindedness among the inmates of eighty-one of the county homes in the state. Investigations by Dr. Harry W. Crane, Director of the Bureau of Mental Hygiene and Health of the State Board of Charities and Public Welfare, indicate that these figures are approximately correct as to definitely recognizable feeble-mindedness. Dr. Crane examined all the white inmates in seven county homes and twenty-eight white inmates in another county home. These county homes were selected in every section of the state. In the case of feeble-mindedness, definitely recognizable as such, the examinations showed about ten per cent more than was reported by the superintendents. So there are perhaps approximately seven hundred feeble-minded inmates, who may be definitely classified as such, in the county homes of the state. One hundred and seventeen insane persons were in the county homes in eighty-one counties, according to the reports on this item. But in the seven county homes studied by him, Dr. Crane found two and one-half times as many insane as indicated in the reports. If this ratio holds for the state, there are more than three hundred insane in county homes in North Carolina. Of these, fifty-five were forcibly confined in their rooms or in cells. Sixty-four cases of epilepsy were reported. Five of the epileptics were forcibly confined. Of the one hundred and twenty-six persons tested by Dr. Crane, two were epileptics; one was a drug addict; eighteen showed some abnormal mental condition, but the form of abnormality was not determined; and fifteen, for one reason or another, could not be tested.

11. A BLIND INSANE MAN

Only five of one hundred and twenty-six were adjudged normal mentally. From the data available it appears a conservative estimate to say that 85 per cent of the inmates of the county homes of the state are mentally abnormal.

Two-thirds of the inmates of county homes have never been married. In 1922 there were fifty-nine married couples, two hundred and sixty-seven widows, and one hundred and eighty widowers.

Forty-six counties reported having no children as inmates. The remaining thirty-nine counties had a total of seventy-nine children under sixteen years of age. The ages of fifty-one of these children were given. Twenty-seven, or 53 per cent, ranged in age from one year or less to five years. Sixteen, or 31 per cent, were between the ages of six and eleven; and eight, or 16 per cent, were between the ages of twelve and fifteen years. Of seventy-nine children, thirty-seven, or about half, were adjudged by those making the report to be definitely feeble-minded; and some of the children, too small as yet to be classified in regard to mental status, were the children of feeble-minded mothers and therefore probably feeble-minded themselves.

In addition to the seventy-nine children who were regular inmates, three counties reported a total of eight boys serving sentences at the county homes as juvenile delinquents.

Forty-two children were reported as having been born in the county homes in the year 1921, some still being inmates and some having died or having been taken away from the homes and put in other institutions or otherwise cared for. Of these forty-two births, thirty-four were illegitimate. In the cases of nine illegitimate children, it was reported that conception took place while the mother was at the county home, and in two instances it was believed that the former superintendents of the home were the fathers.

Most of the counties have failed to make provision for anything approaching adequate medical attention for the inmates of their county homes. The 1922 survey showed more than four hundred or approximately one-fourth of the entire number to be sick. A much larger number doubtless need medical attention. Many should be in regular medical hospitals. Of the four hundred and forty-one reported chronically ill, thirty-nine had tuberculosis; forty-seven were suffering from either gonorrhea or syphilis; twenty were wholly paralyzed and one hundred and thirty-two partially paralyzed; twenty-four were afflicted with cancer. Forty-one out of eighty-three counties reporting on this item say that the doctor comes only when called. In forty-two he is supposed to make regular visits as well. In fifteen he comes less often than once a week; in twenty-one, once a week; and in five, more often than once a week. Thirty-three counties report physical examinations before admission. But examinations are often of the most perfunctory sort. Superintendents of county homes with little supervision, on the other hand, buy and administer large quantities of drugs and nostrums including in some instances opium and its derivatives. In several counties the bill for drugs assumes astonishing proportions.

Usually there are no special facilities for the care of

12. Breeding Places for the Feeble-Minded

the sick. Very few of the homes have even a practical nurse. Hospital wards, equipped as such, are almost non-existent. In the majority of the homes it is not possible adequately to segregate the sick from the well. There are cases of horrible neglect and of brutally crude methods of treatment.[15] Usually the superintendent, or more often his wife, gives the sick such attention as he or she knows how to give and as a multitude of other duties will permit.

In the cases of forty-six counties the statements regarding physical diseases or defects were reported as based on the diagnosis of a reputable physician; in twenty-five cases, as simply the opinion of those in charge of the homes or of the county superintendents of public welfare; fourteen reports did not state whether or not the answers were based on a physician's diagnosis. In six reports there was a question mark after the figures reporting tuberculosis; in seven reports there was a question mark after the figures given on venereal disease; and in some, no figures, simply question marks, were given in regard to these diseases.

The following extract from a recent report of the

[15] In one county home the chronically sore feet of an inmate became so badly infected that the superintendent thought the only remedy was amputation. The county physician promised to go out to see about the old man but neglected to do so. The superintendent finally decided to act. With a butcher's knife and a handsaw he performed the operation. The man survived the operation and lived for a year or two. It is reported that the Superintendent presented a bill for five dollars for the operation to the county commissioners and they paid it. An account of this affair may be found in *The Survey* for September 6, 1919.

grand jury of Guilford County calls attention to a condition that is typical of even the better county homes:

> The grand jury finds that the county home is in splendid condition with one exception. The grand jury most emphatically advises that additional arrangements and precautions be made for the segregation of the inmates of the home that are infected with venereal diseases.[16]

There is usually, perhaps, an honest effort to furnish to inmates of county homes a sufficient quantity of such food as the wife of the superintendent knows how to prepare or has been accustomed to herself. This does not mean that inmates of all county homes are properly fed. In many of the homes they are not. Vegetables, as has been observed elsewhere, are not supplied as constantly or in as great variety as is desirable or practicable. County home farms produce practically no meat except hog meat, which is produced by a considerable number, and the average county home table knows no other except on rare occasions. "Wouldn't it be possible for us to have just a bit of red meat once in a while?" begged an intelligent Negro girl, in an advanced stage of tuberculosis, of the chairman of the board of county commissioners in a certain county. This county farm contains one hundred and seventy-five acres. The county has no livestock on this land. No provision has been made by the county to insure a supply of milk or of eggs. There is not an adequate supply of either. "The inmates of our county home are as well fed as the average

[16] *Greensboro Daily News*, August 4, 1927.

family in the county," declared a member of a board of county commissioners in another county. That morning the inmates of that county home each had for breakfast two slices of fat bacon fried, one tablespoonful of molasses, three biscuits, and coffee. This home is in one of the finest diversified farming sectons in North Carolina. The commissioner simply did not know.

Section 1337, Consolidated Statutes of North Carolina, reads:

The keeper or superintendent in charge of each county home in North Carolina, or the board of county commissioners in each county where there is no county home, shall keep a record book showing the following: Name, age, sex, and race of each inmate; date of entrance or discharge; mental and physical condition; cause of admission; family relation and condition; date of death if in the home; cost of supplies and per capita expense per month; amount of crops and value, and such other information as may be required by the board of county commissioners or the State Board of Charities and Public Welfare. Such report to be filed annually on or before the first Monday of December of each year.

No county in the state in 1922 was keeping this record. Most of the county homes have some sort of record of the inmates, usually giving the name, the date of admission, and that of discharge or death. No county, it seems, keeps a per capita cost account record or a record of the amount and value of crops.

The short period treated in this chapter has been marked by comparatively great activity in the building of new county homes of a very greatly improved type. The State Board of Charities and Public Welfare has been very active in its efforts to improve conditions—

fearless in the exposure of bad conditions and untiring in its efforts to educate the public to the possibility of better methods. Improvements, it is true, have taken a somewhat different direction from that favored by the Board. Its insistence on better care for indoor paupers has been accompanied by repeated statements of the conviction that the number of almshouse inmates should be still further decreased with the development of social technique and that district institutions should therefore supplant county homes. The board has succeeded in arousing public interest in better institutions but not in overcoming local prejudices and county pride. A few advances, which have already been pointed out and which will be appraised more fully in the succeeding chapter, may be the beginnings of a new era in the administration of poor relief in the state.

There has developed in several of the counties greater care in the investigation of applicants for admission to the homes. Boards of county commissioners have been more and more inclined to rely on the county superintendent of public welfare in this matter. A few counties have employed registered nurses or nurses with some training as a part of the county home staff. But in general the county home remains a dumping place for the wrecks of our civilization—a place to which society can remove from its sight its failures and so forget them.

CHAPTER VI

ADMINISTRATION OF OUTDOOR RELIEF BY COUNTY SUPERINTENDENTS OF PUBLIC WELFARE

ABOUT thirty-four hundred people in North Carolina receive outdoor relief from county funds. For this purpose an aggregate of $175,000 a year is spent. Until very recently there has been little or no effort to supervise the outdoor poor in this state. Practices adopted from England in Colonial days have continued to the present. There have been no facilities for supervision. The wardens of the poor of the earlier period had little training or time for such supervision. The county commissioners of more recent years at best could only listen to appeals for aid and use their best judgment, usually without investigation, as to whether aid should be given. Sometimes the appeal has been made on political grounds—the person applying for aid votes right, or a cross-roads merchant conceives the idea of getting some of a delinquent purchaser's bills paid. And sometimes this same cross-roads merchant forgets to report when his customer dies, and goes on drawing the pittance from the county. Sometimes a person in real need is placed on the poor list; the reason for aid later ceases to exist, but he goes on drawing his monthly or quarterly allowance from the county. The amount paid has usually been very small— one to five dollars per month. The effect of such a system has been bad. It has tended not only to lower the stand-

ard of the administration of county government and to
encourage petty graft, but to pauperize at the same time
the one to whom the grant is made.

A few boards of county commissioners, recognizing
the evils of the system, have abolished outdoor relief
entirely and require all persons receiving aid from the
county to go to the county home. A much larger number
now require that all new cases be investigated by the
county superintendent of public welfare, and aid is given
only on his recommendation. A number of counties have
directed the superintendent also to check the entire list
of those to whom relief is given. Considerable numbers
of persons who are dead, who have moved to other counties or other states, or who no longer need help, have
been dropped from the list. In one small county the
saving thus effected amounted to several hundred dollars
a year. In another county twenty-five were dropped within
the first year after the matter was placed under the
supervision of the superintendent of public welfare.

The law provides that the county superintendent of
public welfare shall "have, under control of the county
commissioners, the care and supervision of the poor, and
administer the poor fund."[1] Just how much power the
General Assembly intended should be delegated to the
superintendents of public welfare is not very clear from
the wording of this act. Various boards of county commissioners have apparently interpreted it in various ways.
A reasonable construction, it seems, would be that the
commissioners should in consultation with the superintendent determine the general policy of the county in

[1] *Consolidated Statutes of North Carolina*, sec. 5017.

regard to the relief of the poor and fix the maximum sum available for this purpose. The details of the administration of such fund under the general policy agreed upon would be left to the superintendent of public welfare. This is approximately the policy adopted by several counties. Other boards of commissioners have continued to ignore the law and still attempt to administer the poor funds themselves without the aid of the superintendent of public welfare. In a county whose capital is one of the large cities in the state, the county commissioners not only employ a superintendent of public welfare, but provide, without rent, an office in the county court house for the secretary of the associated charities of the city. Yet this same board of commissioners still doles out pittances to the poor as if these agencies did not exist. Between these two extremes there are various intermediate positions. Sometimes the commissioners continue to grant aid to what is known as a regular or permanent list of paupers, while they give to the superintendent of public welfare a fund for emergency cases and for the aid of such as may be in temporary distress.

This slowness on the part of county commissioners to give up a duty that they have never been able to perform efficiently is due in part to the fact that it has been found possible so to distribute even the pittances given to the poor as to increase the power and enhance the prestige of the commissioners making the grants. A small monthly allowance to a member of a certain family may insure the control of several votes; or the appointment of a certain cross-roads merchant as "agent" for several persons to whom doles from the county poor fund are granted may make the merchant a valuable political supporter of the commissioner who secured his appointment.

The force of custom, also, has retarded acceptance of the new plan. Recently in a county which supports a staff of welfare workers composed of a superintendent and several assistants, a citizen came before the board of county commissioners to say that an aged man was in great need of assistance. The county commissioners discussed the case in a sympathetic manner and finally delegated the superintendent of the county home to visit the old man and decide whether he should be taken to the county home or given aid in his own home. They apparently had forgotten for the moment or were ignorant of the fact that they were supporting a group of social workers whose duty it is under the law to investigate just such cases.

A few instances will show at once some phases of the workings of the old methods and the value of investigation by the county superintendent of public welfare. When a superintendent of public welfare checked up on the twenty-odd persons on the outdoor poor-list in a small county he found that one man on the list was working in West Virginia in connection with a coal mine at good wages. He found further that this man a few months before had been employed as a laborer in the construction of a public road, drawing directly from the county full wages as a laborer at the same time that he was drawing a monthly allowance from the county poor fund as a pauper. Some years before, this man had lost a foot and perhaps had needed temporary aid. Once on the poor-list no one noticed that after his recovery he was able, in spite of his handicap, to do more manual labor than the ordinary man. He was still a young man. The small allowance had already gone far toward pauperizing him. When the allowance to him was discontinued, he first tried to get it renewed, and when he found this impossible, set about getting his father, for whose welfare he had not before shown any great solicitude, placed on the poor-list.

Another man on the poor-list of this county was at the time of the investigation working as a timber-cutter for a lumber company at three dollars and thirty cents a day. A few weeks before he had been employed by a contractor laying pavement in the street in front of the court house. This man, also still young, had a stiff knee. There may have been a time when he needed temporary aid. At the time in question, although handicapped somewhat, he was able to earn full wages as a laborer.

In another county the county superintendent of public welfare found that one man who had been out of the county two and a half years and dead six months was still on the outdoor pauper list. His quarterly check was going to his "agent," a man worth a hundred thousand dollars. A second man, forty-eight years old, was a clerk in a store at a good salary. Four years before he had been thought to have tuberculosis and was placed on the outdoor poor list. His voucher was going to the same wealthy citizen referred to above and was credited on the clerk's house rent. Roger Williams, a cripple in need of aid, had been placed on the list some years before the investigation in 1923. Within two years he received but two quarterly vouchers. The same wealthy citizen was drawing the money from the county but was rendering absolutely no service to the pauper for whom the money was intended. One woman on the list had lived in another county for three years. Her brother was drawing her allowance. And finally one enterprising woman was getting money from the poor funds of three counties.

In 1922 Robeson County was spending $12,500 a year in pittances distributed among two hundred and fifty outdoor poor, when the matter was placed in the hands of an energetic superintendent of public welfare. The first year she managed to strike twenty-five names from the list; but people may be pauperized even by doles of from one to five dollars a month, when such allowances have been continued long enough. It was hard to show these people that they could get along without aid. Her next step, therefore, was to induce the county to build a modern county home. When this was opened, applicants for aid were required to go to the "home." On June 9, 1925, the county superintendent of public welfare wrote:

On March 1, I had 248 paupers outside of the county home, and 20 in the county home. Paid out $961.50 to the outside pauper list. June 1, I had 100 paupers on the outside pauper list and 39 in the county home. I made a survey of the county, visited each pauper, and if he could be placed in the county home I did so. If not I cut his pension.[2]

The reduction in the number of paupers on the outdoor list continued after the date of this letter. The average

[2] Letter in files of North Carolina State Board of Charities and Public Welfare, dated June 9, 1925.

daily number of inmates in the county home for the year ending November 30, 1925, was fifty. At the end of the year the number was forty-six. The average number for the year of persons aided each month from the outdoor poor funds was fifty-two. The total amount paid to outdoor poor for the year was $2,534. Here was a reduction of two hundred in the number of outdoor paupers, and of $10,000 per year in the total amount spent for such relief. The total number of paupers, indoor and outdoor, was reduced from two hundred and sixty-five in 1922 to one hundred in 1925. The total cost of relief, however, was of course increased, as the operation of the county home at the end of the year was about $2,000 a month. Commenting on the situation, the superintendent of public welfare said, "Our aim is to place all paupers in the county home and have no outdoor relief except emergency cases."[3] While the application of the old "work house test" can hardly be approved today, it is evident that drastic action in regard to the outdoor list in this county was necessary.

Cherokee County also has made history in the administration of outdoor relief. In the summer of 1924 public welfare work was organized in this county in the extreme southwestern corner of the state. Prior to this time poor relief had been administered in the old haphazard way. In 1922 forty names appeared on the outdoor poor list.[4] By 1924 the number had increased to

[3] Report to State Board of Charities and Public Welfare September 8, 1926.

[4] County Report files, North Carolina State Board of Charities and Public Welfare.

seventy. Under the new plan all requests for aid from the county are turned over to the superintendent of public welfare. She decides whether outdoor or indoor relief shall be given. In this way many who might under the old system get on the county pension roll are eliminated. In September, 1926, for instance, of nine applicants only two were granted aid from county funds. The list of seventy, moreover, has been reduced to four or five.[5] The county home population has not been greatly increased. For the three years, 1922 to 1925, the number of inmates remained constantly at eight. Late in 1926 there were eleven.

In Vance County the number receiving aid outside the county hospital, as has been stated in another chapter, has been reduced, under the administration of the county superintendent of public welfare, about one-half. At the same time more than two-thirds of the inmates of the county home have been transferred to the outdoor list. The amount spent on outdoor relief in this county in 1922 was $2,258; in 1925 it was $1,451.[6]

In most of the counties, however, no such progress toward the solution of this problem has been made. In quite a number a little more care, perhaps, is taken in investigating new cases of application for aid. In quite as large a group no progress has been made in the policy or technique of poor relief since colonial days. For the

[5] C. W. Edwards, *County Government and County Affairs in Cherokee County*, 1927. MS., Institute for Research in Social Science, University of North Carolina.

[6] North Carolina State Board of Charities and Public Welfare, files.

biennial period of 1924 to 1926, seventy-four counties reported to the State Board of Charities and Public Welfare on outdoor relief. In these seventy-four counties 2,650 persons were receiving aid outside county homes. For this purpose there was an expenditure of $135,800. The same counties in 1921 were giving aid to 2,975 outdoor poor. They spent for that purpose the same year $111,289. The whole amount spent for 1921 was $156,750, and the whole number receiving aid was a few more than 3,800.[7] If the figures for these seventy-four counties hold relatively for the entire state, somewhat more than 3,400 persons received aid in 1925 to the total amount of approximately $175,000.

In addition to the relief from county funds, many towns and cities also administer outdoor relief from their own public funds. Reports from the twenty-seven cities in the state with populations of five thousand or more show $167,834.15 spent for purposes classified as relief work. The total amount spent by towns and cities, therefore, is as large as that spent by the counties for outdoor relief. The figures, however, are by no means strictly compàrable. Several cities state that they classify together funds spent for outdoor relief and for the support of hospitals. One city, Durham, classifies together "hospitals, charities, libraries, etc." Winston-Salem states that she spent $35,000 "for the relief of the poor through the City Memorial Hospital, a city-owned institution," and $5,000 additional through the city health depàrtment. None of this perhaps should be listed as outdoor

[7] North Carolina State Board of Charities and Public Welfare, *Biennial Report, 1920-22*, pp. 76-77.

poor relief. In fact, in every case where a city reports the expenditure of several thousand dollars for relief work, the larger part seems to have been for the support of hospitals and similar forms of welfare work.

The apparent diversity in the classification of expenditures makes any comparison of one city with another particularly difficult. This is especially true of the larger cities. Three cities with population of five to six thousand and one with a population of twelve thousand report nothing spent for poor relief. The charter of one—Washington—prohibits the expenditure of public funds for "any purpose other than actual operating expenses."

A very few of the cities administer poor relief through the county superintendent of public welfare. At least one uses the Salvation Army, another the local charity organization society, and so on. On the whole, public relief work in the towns and cities seems quite as poorly organized as in the counties.

Such figures as are available seem to indicate that under the partial supervision by county superintendents of public welfare that now exists, there has been a decrease in the number of persons receiving outside aid, but an increase in the amount expended for this purpose. The decrease in numbers for the four years from 1921 to 1925 amounted to somewhat more than 10 per cent. The increase in the total sums spent annually for the same period amounted to more than 20 per cent.[8] Both of these facts indicate that the counties are slowly heading in the right direction. It is evident to anyone who has

[8] North Carolina State Board of Charities and Public Welfare, *Special Bulletin No. 4, 1925*, p. 57.

given the matter the most casual thought not only that more careful selection and greater supervision of the cases to be aided is needed, but also that for those who are aided the grants must be much larger than has been customary.

From the data available it appears that the tendencies indicated are due to reforms in a very limited number of counties. In the great majority a century has witnessed no material change in the policy or technique of outdoor relief. Pittances are doled out to a group of the poor who receive the first allowance perhaps with little or no investigation as to its necessity and who continue as pensioners on the county with no supervision. No one apparently thinks the matter worth serious attention, perhaps because the amount given to each individual is so small. In 1921 the amounts given ranged from seventy-five cents to thirty dollars a month. In fifty-seven counties the amount most commonly given was less than five dollars. In ten counties it was less than two dollars and in sixteen others just two dollars. In only three counties did the modal grant reach ten dollars per month.[9] For the two years of 1924 and 1925, in seventy-four counties from which one or more reports for the period are in the files of the State Board of Charities and Public Welfare, 1781 individuals received less than five dollars a month and only one hundred and fifteen more than ten dollars.

There is no uniformity as to the extent of outdoor relief in the different counties. In a group of six counties having a population of fifteen thousand each the number

[9] North Carolina State Board of Charities and Public Welfare, *Biennial Report, 1920-22*, p. 76.

receiving aid from the county ranged from eleven to fifty-five. In a second group of eight counties with populations of eighteen to twenty thousand, the smallest number receiving outdoor relief was seven and the largest eighty. In another group of counties with populations from thirty to thirty-five thousand the number of outdoor paupers varied from eleven to eighty-five.[10]

It is not a pleasing picture that is presented by the story of the administration of outdoor relief in North Carolina. There is widespread pauperization of the recipients of aid unscientifically administered and hopelessly insufficient in amount. There is political exploitation of the poor funds, and there is graft. County commissioners ignorant of the law, or unwilling to give up any of their prerogatives, or carried on by the inertia of custom, fail to avail themselves of the services of the county superintendent of public welfare. Superintendents of public welfare have so many duties that they often neglect this, perhaps the least attractive of them all. There are enough counties, however, in which intelligent social work is being introduced into this field to give ground for the hope that this is the beginning of the end of the unsupervised outdoor poor-list.

One important development in the relief of the poor in the state, very unlike ordinary outdoor relief and yet closely related to it, remains to be considered. The most important step yet taken by the state in the relief of poverty and the prevention of pauperism was the enactment in 1923 of a mothers' aid law. At the close of the

[10] North Carolina State Board of Charities and Public Welfare, files.

fiscal year ending June 30, 1926, seventy-one counties had chosen to take advantage of this law. For the biennial period ending on that date, $107,834.40 was expended from state and county funds for the aid of capable though indigent mothers with young children.[11] One-half of this amount was appropriated by the counties participating. Increased appropriation by the state makes it probable that this sum will be practically doubled for the next two years. This form of aid is treated at more length in the following chapter on the care of the dependent child.

It is in this change of point of view to the idea of the prevention of pauperism, which is coupled with the ideal of the preservation of the home ties for the child in the mothers' aid policy, and in the influence of this new policy of relief with its new methods, that there is hope for the future of outdoor poor relief in North Carolina. If the state insists upon careful investigation of applicants for mothers' aid and careful supervision of the expenditure of the funds granted to mothers of this superior class of the poor, may it not occur to county commissioners that there should be even more careful supervision of the funds granted for the aid of the less capable poor? It is by no means impracticable that the administration of ordinary poor relief should approximate the standards set by the State Board of Charities and Public Welfare for the administration of mothers' aid.

[11] North Carolina State Board of Charities and Public Welfare, *Biennial Report, 1924-26*, p. 58-59.

CHAPTER VII

DEPENDENT CHILDREN

THE earliest attempt at the care of dependent children by governmental supervision in North Carolina was by apprenticeship. As early as 1695 the following record was made:

Upon ye Petition of Hon^{ell} Thomas Harvey es^{qr} Ordered ye W^m ye son of Timothy Bead late of the County of Albemarle Dec^d being left destitute be bound unto ye sd Thomas Harvey es^{qr} and Sarah his wife untill he be at ye age twenty one years and the said Thomas Harvey to teach him to read.[1]

From the records of the Perquimans Precinct Court for the January, 1699, term:

Jonathan Taylor And William Taylor Orfens Being Left destressed ordered that they be bound to William Long And Sarah His Wife Till they Come of Age.

Thomas Tailer Orfen Being Left destressed ordered that He be bound to John Lawrence And Hannah his wife till he Comes of Age.

Mare Tayler Orfen being Left destressed ordered that he be bound to ffrancis ffoster And Hannah his Wife till he Comes of Age.

Thomas Hallom Orfen being left destressed ordered that he be bound to ffrancis ffoster And Hannah his Wife till he Comes of Age.[2]

In 1702 in the records of this court this item appears:

Martha Plato Binds Hir daughter Hester to Capt

[1] *Colonial Records of North Carolina*, I, 448.
[2] *Ibid.*, p. 522.

James Coles And Mary His Wife till Shee comes of Age
or married Shee Being now Sixe years of Age And At the
Experation of Hir time to Alow to ye Garle According to
the Custom of ye Cuntry.[3]

In the record of this court for March 9, 1703, this
entry appears:

Upon a petition of Gabirel Newby for two orphants
left him by Mary Hancock the late wife of Thom^s
Hancocke and proveing the same by the oathes of Eliz.
Stenward and her daughter the Court doe agree to bind
them unto him he Ingaging & promising before the Courte
to doe his endeavours to learne the boy the trade of a
wheelright and likewise give him at the expiration of his
time one ear old heifer and to ye girle at her freedome
one Cow and Calfe besides the Custome of the Country
and has promised at ye next orphans Court to Sign In-
dentures for that effect.[4]

The first apprenticeship law enacted by the legislature
of North Carolina, it appears, was passed in 1715. Up
to this time the colonists had evidently adapted the principles and customs of English law to their use. The law
of 1715 defined, therefore, a law already in force. This
law provided that orphans should be apprenticed only
by the precinct court; that all orphans should be educated
according to their rank and degree, out of the means of
their property, if that were sufficient and that destitute
orphans should be bound apprentice to some handicraft
trade.[5]

In a letter from Governor Gabriel Johnston to the
Lords of the Board of Trade, dated December 5, 1735,

[3] *Ibid.*, p. 566.
[4] *Ibid.*, p. 577.
[5] *State Records of North Carolina*, XXIII, 70.

among the notes on the laws of the colony the following appears:

An Act Concerning Orphans.

This law highly unjust and seems designed to encourage and protect unjust guardians who rob their wards, a practice too common in this country.[6]

It seems that the governor's opposition to the practices in regard to orphans extended to the treatment of the children as well as of their estates. At any rate complaints were made that Governor Johnston had released orphans bound by the justices.[7]

In 1755 the Committee on Propositions and Grievances of the colonial assembly recommended that "Grand Jurys in the County Courts have Power to make inquiry into the Abuse of Orphans and their Estates and that Relief in such Cases be had in a summary Way."[8] In the same year the law in regard to orphans was amended to provide that the churchwardens in every parish should furnish to the justices of the orphans court at its annual session the names of all children without guardians; that the guardian should maintain and educate the orphan according to his or her degree; and that indigent orphans should be apprenticed, boys until they were twenty-one and girls until they were eighteen or were married; and that orphans so apprenticed should be trained for some trade or employment and taught to read and write. The court was

[6] *Colonial Records of North Carolina,* IV, 26.
[7] *Colonial Records of North Carolina,* IV, 1118.
[8] *Ibid.,* V, 298.

given power to remove any apprentice if the master did not carry out these terms.[9]

The powers given to the justices of the peace who composed the orphans courts were such as to call forth rather severe criticism from the highest judicial officers of the colony. In 1759 Charles Berry, chief justice, and Thomas Child, attorney-general of the colony, reported that with respect to this law "the jurisdiction that is thereby given to the county courts is not warranted by any similar practice or law in this county, and therefore this act ought in our humble opinion to be repealed."[10] These officials did not state whether it was the powers in regard to the apprenticing children or appointing guardians or the power of removing the child from the master that was objectionable from the point of view of precedent.

In 1760 the law requiring that the churchwardens of every parish present annually to the justices of the orphans court the names of all orphans without guardians was reënacted.[11] In 1762 this law was amended by transferring the duty of reporting children without guardians from the churchwardens to the grand jury. At the same time the provisions as to apprenticeship were extended to include "all free base-born children" and "every such female child being a mulatto or mustee."[12]

The apprenticeship system remained in North Carolina as an important method of providing for orphans until

[9] *State Records of North Carolina*, XXV, 323.
[10] *Colonial Records of North Carolina*, VI, 20.
[11] *State Records of North Carolina*, XXV, 419.
[12] *Ibid.*, XXIII, 581.

the passage of the juvenile court law in 1919. After the Revolution the power of apprenticing children was vested in the county courts.[13] It was transferred after the Civil War to the clerk of the superior court in each county.[14] The Code of 1888 provided that the clerks of the superior courts in their respective counties should bind out as apprentices:

(1)   All orphans whose estates are of so small value that no person will educate and maintain them for the profits thereof;

(2)   All infants whose fathers have deserted their families and been absent for one year, leaving them without sufficient support;

(3)   All infants (not living with the father) whose mother has secured to her such property as the infants may thereafter acquire, provided the clerk deems it improper to permit such infants to remain with the mother;

(4)   All infants who make application to the board of commissioners of the county for relief out of the funds for the poor, and such fact is certified by the board to the clerk;

(5)   All infants whose parents do not habitually employ their time in some honest, industrious occupation.[15]

The frequency of apprenticing or "binding out" children decreased of course with the rise of orphanages and the later organization of a child-placing society.

The county almshouse has throughout its history, as already pointed out, cared for a considerable number of children. Some of the early acts providing for the establishment of poorhouses in North Carolina specifically

[13] *Laws of North Carolina, 1821*, I, 215.
[14] *The Code of North Carolina, 1888*, sec. 9.
[15] *Ibid.*, sec. 2.

stated that these institutions should receive poor persons
who because of old age, infirmity, or infancy were unable to sustain themselves. In 1870 the State Board of
Charities listed among the inmates of the poor-house
"the orphan and the child of poverty, for whom beats no
heart warm with the kindly emotions," and among the
shortcomings of the institution, the fact that no provision
is made for teaching the children gathered there.[16] In
1891 eighty-one children were reported in county homes
and in 1892 one hundred fourteen.[17] In 1922 there were·
still seventy-nine children in these institutions.[18]

One of the least creditable phases in the history of the
care of dependent children in North Carolina is that
dealing with those who have been so unfortunate as to
fall into the county almshouses. Usually they have been
given away by county commissioners to anyone who
would take them. Often there has not been the formality
of a legal apprenticeship. "In this connection," wrote
the secretary of the State Board of Charities in 1891, "it
is not improper to suggest that legislation be enacted to
provide for closer supervision of the children bound from
time to time, as they are supposed to be old enough, from
our County Homes."[19]

At a rather early date in the history of the state in-

[16] North Carolina State Board of Public Charities, *Report,
1870*, pp. 7-8.
[17] North Carolina State Board of Public Charities, *Report,
1891-92*, pp. 10, 290.
[18] North Carolina State Board of Charities and Public Welfare,
Poor Relief in North Carolina, Special Bulletin No. 4, 1925, p. 18.
[19] North Carolina State Board of Public Charities, *Report,
1891-92*, p. 9.

terest was shown in the establishment of orphanages for
the care of children. In 1812 the Newbern Female
Charitable Society for the relief of the poor and the
education of poor female children was incorporated by
act of the General Assembly.[20] In 1813 the Female Orphan
Asylum Society of Fayetteville was incorporated and
authorized to take under its care and protection, by and
with the consent of the wardens of the poor of Cumberland County, children who were destitute of both parents
and who might become chargeable to the county,

which said children they the said society shall be allowed
to board, clothe, and educate, until the society conceive
them properly qualified to bind out to proper trades or
professions, and whenever said society so conceives, it is
hereby authorized, by and with the consent of the county
court of Cumberland, to bind out such children in the
same manner as the county court have heretofore done.[21]

The orphanage as an established institution, however,
developed in North Carolina in the period following the
Civil War. The constitution of 1868 had provided that
"there shall also, as soon as practicable, be measures
devised by the state for the establishment of one or more
orphan houses, where destitute orphans may be cared
for, educated and taught some business or trade."[22]

In 1872 St. John's College, Oxford, the property of
the Masonic fraternity, was converted by the action of
the Grand Lodge into an institution "for the protection,
training and education" of indigent orphans of North
Carolina. "The orphanage which thus came into being

[20] *Public Laws of North Carolina, 1812,* chap. 70.
[21] *Public Laws of North Carolina, 1813,* chap. 44.
[22] *North Carolina Constitution,* art. XI, sec. 8.

was the first institution of its kind in the state and one of the first in the South.[23]   It certainly marked the beginning of the building of a number of such institutions in North Carolina. The last report of the State Board of Charities and Public Welfare lists twenty-three orphanages and six local institutions for the temporary care of children.[24] In 1924 there were in these institutions, exclusive of county detention homes, 3,719 children.[25]

Of the twenty-three orphanages in the state, seventeen are under the control of the various religious denominations and of four fraternal orders. Under the influence of these organizations the orphanage idea has taken strong hold upon the public mind, and many enthusiastic supporters of church or lodge have been accustomed to believe that the greatest good fortune that can befall the average child is to be sent to an orphanage. Scores of children, therefore, are hurried off thither who might with a little intelligent effort be placed in the homes of relatives or in other suitable foster homes.[26] The orphanages themselves have promoted this spirit and have often rather strenuously opposed any suggestion that there could be any better arrangement for an orphan

[23] *Historical Sketch of Oxford Orphan Asylum*, p. 6.

[24] North Carolina State Board of Charities and Public Welfare, *Biennial Report, 1924-26*, pp. 17-22.

[25] North Carolina State Board of Charities and Public Welfare, *Biennial Report, 1922-24*, p. 40.

[26] In closing a small Negro orphanage in 1924 the State Board of Charities and Public Welfare found it practicable to place nine-tenths of the children with parents or relatives. *Biennial Report 1922-24*, p. 40. See also p. 159.

than to send him to an orphanage. It is not surprising, therefore, to find that, in 1924, of 3,719 children in orphanages, less than one-third, 1,140, were full orphans; and that 353 had both parents living.[27]

The state has complied, in a measure at least, with the constitutional requirement by subsidizing two orphanages, the Oxford Orphanage, controlled by the Masons, and the Oxford Orphanage, Colored. The legislature has further met the requirement implied in that section of the state constitution which created a board of charities, by making it the duty of the State Board of Charities and Public Welfare to inspect and make report on private orphanages. The law provided further that orphanages must be licensed annually by the State Board. When the Board became somewhat insistent in its campaign of education toward higher standards, certain orphanage superintendents became alarmed and resentful. After a fight in the legislature in which appeals to fraternal loyalty, religious prejudice, and political factionalism played an important part, the General Assembly of 1925 repealed the requirement of an annual license, as that requirement applies to orphanages with property holdings worth $60,000 or more.[28] Under the law as thus modified only two orphanages are required to have a license to operate. The power of inspection and of requiring annual reports remains.

Child-placing in some form has existed in North Carolina since the earliest days of her history. The

[27] North Carolina State Board of Charities and Public Welfare, *Biennial Report, 1922-24*, p. 40.

[28] *Public Laws of North Carolina, 1925*, chap. 90.

apprenticeship system has already been discussed. This was supplemented later by adoption, by which from time to time children have become legal members in the families of foster parents. A growing recognition of the fact that many children may be placed in homes with mutual benefit to both the homes and the children, on a very different basis from that implied in the old apprenticeship system or the custom of giving children away from county homes by boards of county commissioners, led to the organization of the Children's Home Society of North Carolina, Incorporated. Since its work began, twenty-five years ago, the society has placed in foster homes approximately twenty-five hundred children.[29]

The operations of the Children's Home Society have been both facilitated and supplemented by the organization of the state's system of public welfare on a county unit basis. County superintendents of public welfare have become, for all practical purposes, agents of the society both in referring children to the society and in investigating prospective homes. On the financial side, various boards of county commissioners have appropriated money from public funds for the support of the society. These donations for the year 1926, as stated in a letter from the superintendent, amounted to $6,673.37. In addition, the county superintendents of public welfare working with the Juvenile Court Judges have placed many children— both in temporary and in permanent homes.

The juvenile court law assumes also that the State

[29]·Annual Report, 1926.

Board of Charities and Public Welfare will undertake the placing of children in foster homes,[30] but the board has not yet entered this field except in an advisory capacity and as an aid to county superintendents of public welfare and other agencies in adjusting difficult cases.

The state from time to time has made provision for the care and training of special classes of handicapped children who otherwise in many instances would become county charges. As early as 1845 the state had made some provision for the education of indigent blind and deaf children.[31] The succeeding legislature made provision for the establishment of a state institution for this purpose.[32] From this has developed the school for the white deaf at Morganton and the schools for the white blind and for the Negro blind and deaf at Raleigh. Attendance of all blind and deaf children in the state is now compulsory.

For many years these were the only classes of handicapped children provided for by the state. In 1911 an institution for the care and training of the feeble-minded was provided for.[33] This institution, known as the Caswell Training School, has an enrollment of about four hundred, most of whom are children.[34] Although entirely inadequate in size to meet the demands upon it, its capacity has not been increased within the last two years. The General Assembly of 1927, however, made provision

[30] *Consolidated Statutes of North Carolina*, sec. 5047, subsec. 3.
[31] *Public Laws of North Carolina, 1844-45*, chap. 37.
[32] *Public Laws of North Carolina, 1846-47*, chap. 48.
[33] *Public Laws of North Carolina, 1911*, chap. 67.
[34] Caswell Training School, *Biennial Report, 1924-26.*

for the building of two additional dormitories and one colony house.

The institution, however, has taken a number of white children as well as adults who otherwise must have become county charges. There is no state provision for the care of feeble-minded Negroes except that they are occasionally committed to the hospital for the Negro insane.

In 1917 the legislature made provision for an orthopedic hospital.[35] The hospital was opened at Gastonia in 1921. This institution, known as the North Carolina Orthopedic Hospital, has corrected, for hundreds of children, handicaps which otherwise would have rendered them physically helpless for life or would have greatly impaired their ability to earn a living. Within the biennial period of 1924 to 1926, 561 children were cared for.[36] Within this period also a ward for Negro children was opened at the hospital. Through the coöperation of the hospital with the State Board of Charities and Public Welfare clinics have been held in every section of the state, at which free examinations have been given crippled children. Between April, 1923, and June 30, 1926, twenty-two clinics were held and 1,149 children examined.[37] The institution is beyond doubt a powerful agency in the prevention of dependency.

Finally, perhaps the most important step yet taken by the state in the care of the dependent child was the

[35] *Public Laws of North Carolina, 1917,* chap. 199.
[36] North Carolina State Board of Charities and Public Welfare, *Biennial Report, 1924-26,* p. 67.
[37] *Ibid.,* p. 62.

enactment in 1923 of a mothers' aid law. This law makes possible financial aid for mothers with children under fourteen years old, from a fund provided jointly by the state and the county and administered under the supervision of the State Board of Charities and Public Welfare. On June 30, 1926, the director reported 264 active cases of mothers' aid involving 984 children.[38]

The report shows that during the biennial period fifty-eight new cases were added and forty dropped. Of these forty mothers it is significant, in contrast with the usual effect of the older type of poor relief, that seventeen had become self-supporting. Thirteen others had married again.[39] The effect of the operation of the law in a case of a mother still receiving aid is illustrated by the following case as reported by the director:

A young farmer died of cancer in the spring of 1925, leaving his wife and three children, with practically no resources. A small life insurance policy gave enough money to pay funeral expenses and a few debts. The young mother used the rest for bare necessities and was over-taxing her strength in trying to run the farm.

Now the State stepped in, not with just a few dollars to give relief for a few days, but with a definite plan for the family.

The county superintendent of welfare studied the case, and recommended that the State and county give the mother from the Mothers' Aid fund the sum of twenty-five dollars a month. He made arrangements with some of the woman's relatives, by which she could have part of a house, in a small town, near a good school, which the two older children could attend. As the mother's need

[38] *Ibid.*, p. 52.
[39] *Ibid.*, p. 51.

had been discovered soon after the husband's death, the family was not under-nourished and needed no medical attention. The State Director of Mothers' Aid approved the plan, and the mother was put on the list in November, 1925.

Her plan had been to take in sewing, in the new home. Instead, a place was found for her in a new draping shop, where she works every day making curtains, counterpanes and other household furnishings on an electric machine. The two older children are doing well in school. . . .

Today, less than a year from the time she was given her first check, the mother is almost self-supporting, and it is expected that in a few months she will be entirely so.[40]

The reaction of the orphanages to the mothers' aid program is interesting.

The orphanages of the state are also interested in Mothers' Aid, says the state director. "They have long waiting lists and six of them—Oxford, Thomasville, Presbyterian, Odd Fellows, Methodist Orphanage at Raleigh, and the Pythian—have asked the help of the Division of Child Welfare this last year in investigating homes of children in their institutions with a view of returning children to them if the homes proved able in every way except financially to care for them. Unfortunately because of the fact that all counties where eligible mothers were living, were already using all their State and county funds it is impossible to take them on as Mothers' Aid cases.[41]

For the Odd Fellows' Home forty-nine cases involving one hundred and ten children were considered. In twenty cases involving twenty-three children, the children were

[40] North Carolina State Board of Charities and Public Welfare, *Biennial Report, 1924-26,* p. 54.
[41] *Ibid.,* p. 60.

returned to relatives, in twelve cases to their mothers. Only two good mothers' aid prospects were found, involving seven children. "Eight homes were reported as not of mothers' aid quality." Twenty homes involving sixty-seven children were found unsuitable financially or otherwise for the return of the children. In seven cases involving thirteen children the reports were not in. In this single example the population of an orphanage, it was shown, could be reduced twenty per cent in three months with the possibility of still further reduction when all cases have been thoroughly investigated. The report further raises the interesting question as to the effect on the mother of institutional care of the child. "Several of the cases indicate that the mother, relieved of responsibility, does not care to reassume it even if granted financial aid."[42]

In dealing with the problem of the dependent child, then, North Carolina has come from the old apprenticeship system, supplemented by ordinary outdoor poor relief and from institutional care in the poorhouse, supplemented in turn by the unsupervised giving away of the children in these institutions, to the care of children in orphanages, to the final supplanting of the apprenticeship system by the juvenile court ideal of doing whatever may be best for the child; to the creation of a state-wide, private child-placing agency supplemented by county departments of public welfare; to the definite conviction on the part of the State Board of Charities and Public Welfare that no child should be removed from its home until every effort has been exhausted to make that home func-

[42] *Loc. cit.*

tion as it should; to the inauguration, in this connection, of a policy of mothers' aid from state and county funds; and to the beginning of a realization on the part of the orphanages and of county officials that commitment to an institution should be the last resort in the care of the child.

There is much yet to be desired in this field. Facilities for the care of certain classes of handicapped children are shamefully inadequate. Orphanage standards have not yet been brought up to present day ideals for child-caring institutions. The staff of the Children's Home Society is entirely inadequate for the careful choice of homes in which children are to be placed and the efficient supervision of such homes as are selected. Juvenile courts are usually without trained judges, often without trained workers, and always without adequate staffs. Legislative support of the mothers' aid idea has been at best timid and half-hearted. The work has, therefore, been handicapped seriously both by inadequate funds for the aid of mothers and by an inadequate staff for its supervision. Nevertheless, within the whole scope of relief work, it is in the care of the dependent and the handicapped child that the greatest progress in North Carolina has been made.

CHAPTER VIII

POSSIBLE SOLUTIONS FOR THE PROBLEMS
OF POOR RELIEF

THE problem of the relief of the poor which demands
solution in North Carolina is twofold. For a hundred and
fifty years before the first almshouse was built in the state,
local officials had been granting doles to people who were
adjudged unable to sustain themselves. And after the
poorhouse became an established institution, the method
of aiding a large number of the county's poor outside the
institution continued. Today most counties have both
the County Home for the Aged and Infirm, as the almshouse is now officially called, and the outdoor poor list,
the latter almost always a much larger group than
that in the institution. In the administration of this outdoor relief there has been a beginning of the application
of social casework methods to the investigation of requests for aid. More and more, boards of county commissioners are relying upon the report of the county superintendent of public welfare as to the needs of the ap-
plicant. In practically all cases the amounts granted are
still so small, however, as to be of little real value. The
effect of the system upon those who get on the "list" has
in no material way been changed. Very rarely, apparently, has even the county superintendent of public
welfare conceived of the possibility of using the outdoor
poor funds for the rehabilitation of those who are aided.
It would, of course, be ludicrous to suggest the budgeting

of the family expenditures on an allowance of two or three dollars a month, or to attempt any constructive work on the basis of these doles alone. Here and there, however, as has already been pointed out, a beginning of more scientific methods has been made, and it may not be entirely beyond the bounds of reason to hope that the state's insistence on somewhat adequate grants for mothers' aid cases and on careful planning of the expenditure by the mothers of funds granted may finally suggest to county officials the desirability of the same common-sense methods in dealing with all relief.

When poor relief is mentioned it usually calls up a picture of the county home with its heterogeneous groups of inmates, its squalor, and its unbusinesslike management. The quite general opinion of those who have given the matter serious thought that the almshouse problem is soluble only through a radical change in policy or technique is expressed by the following quotations, one from the state agency charged with the supervision of relief, and the other from a daily newspaper:

Measured by any decent standard of social efficiency the county home is a failure. From the very nature of the problem it could not be a success. The number of paupers in most county homes is so small that it is not economical to maintain them in well-kept county homes.[1]

Whatever we call them, poorhouses are waste.[2]

The first characteristic of the problem of the almshouse which renders it so difficult of solution is the heteroge-

[1] North Carolina State Board of Charities and Public Welfare, *Biennial Report, 1920-22*, p. 63.

[2] *Raleigh Times*, editorial, June 10, 1926.

neous character of the inmates. Writing of almshouses throughout the United States, Harry C. Evans says:

The poorfarm is presumed to be a place, supported by the local community, where the intelligent poor, unable to support themselves, may find comfort in their old age, and for the relief of the intelligent, indigent adults of any age. The general official classificatiton of the inmates, however, is as follows: Paupers, insane, idiots, feeble-minded, blind, deaf mutes, drunkards, drug addicts, sufferers from chronic diseases, criminals, epileptics, children, prostitutes, mothers of illegitimate children. The poor-farm is our human dumping ground into which go our derelicts of every description. Living in this mass of insanity and depravity, this prison place for criminals and the insane, are several thousand children and respectable, intelligent old folk, whose only offense is that they are poor.[3]

These classes are thrown together in institutions in such small numbers as to make classification impracticable. In 1924, twenty-six county homes in North Carolina had fewer than ten inmates. Seventy-one had fewer than twenty-five. Only nine had as many as forty, and only one had more than a hundred.[4]

Neither the public nor the officials responsible for the maintenance of the county home have recognized the nature or the difficulties of the problem with which they are dealing. There are rarely even in the larger institutions facilities for the segregation of the various classes of inmates. Three or four county homes in North Carolina have registered nurses or nurses with some professional

[3] *The American Poorfarm and Its Inmates*, p. 7.
[4] North Carolina State Board of Charities and Public Welfare, *Biennial Report, 1922-24*, p. 76.

training. As many more have "practical" nurses. In all the others no special arrangement is made for the care of sick and feeble inmates.

The superintendent, with help insufficient to look after the inmates alone, is charged often with the management of a farm as well, or more often there is attached to the county home a considerable tract of land from which the superintendent by his own efforts is expected to supplement his meager salary. The superintendent himself is frequently without the ability to manage intelligently either the almshouse or the farm. His financial condition is such that he would be unable to finance the operation of the farm even though he had the intelligence.

The county home is a part of the political spoils system of the county. The superintendent is appointed because he has been useful to the political faction in power, or because he will take the position for less than anyone else and will thus promote a policy of economy to which the county commissioners are committed.

As a remedy for the shortcomings of the county almshouse, many students of the problem within recent years have suggested some sort of consolidation of the smaller units. Discussing the problem from this angle, the *Raleigh Times* suggests a state institution:

It remains the fact that while Wake County has a plentiful supply of the helpless, other counties in this and other Southern States are in the position of having invested much money in Poorhouse buildings and plants, only to find that they have, practically speaking, no poor to care for. It is an age of consolidation, of economy, of efficiency. Why, without relaxing the county obligation to the helpless poor, is there not room for a State home

for the indigent, to which counties could send their poor
and engage for their support? Think of the public buildings and plants—frequently modern to the last gasp and
magnificently equipped—which might thus be used to
other more pressing ends than that of an obligation
which more general prosperity is constantly tending to
repeal![5]

The writer of this editorial has no very intimate ac-
quaintance with the institutions which he is discussing—
his "magnificently equipped" is sufficient evidence; but
he has arrived at the same general conclusion as the
greater number of other students of the problem—that
there must be a larger unit if there is to be economic and
efficient administration of almshouses.

A suggestion more often made by students of the problem is of a district almshouse which would care for
the poor of several counties. Of such a possible solution
Gillin writes:

The district unit would enable the authorities to provide buildings suitable for the classification spoken of
above—separate buildings for hospital use, and cottages
for old couples. It would also permit the hiring of a
high-grade superintendent, and matron for the management of the institution. It would permit the employment
of a regular medical attendant and nurses for the care of
the sick. . . . It would also enable the superintendent to
provide work adapted to the capabilities of those able to
work only in part, because he would have more inmates
and therefore a larger number of able-bodied for whom
he could arrange occupation suited to their needs. Such
a plan would be more economical than the present
plan. . . . Nothing could be more extravagant and inefficient than the present system of county almshouses. This
might be excused if the inmates were securing proper

[5] *Raleigh Times*, June 10, 1926.

care. When, however, the present system involves not only waste of money, but disgraceful care of these helpless paupers, there is nothing to be said in favor of it.[6]

Concerning the same problem the Bureau of Labor Statistics of the United States Department of Labor points out that

In most of the States in which an official body is active in the study and treatment of social problems, the almshouse and almshouse conditions are receiving intelligent consideration as part of those social problems. In practically every one of them the conclusion is the same—that, as the Alabama board says, it is because of the system under which they are operated that conditions have become insufferable, "and a betterment can not be expected until a radical change is inaugurated." There is not only the most universal agreement with the South Carolina board that the establishment of district almshouses, well-planned, well-equipped, and well-managed, with the main idea in mind, the care of the poor, seems to be the most practical and efficient solution of the problem at this time, but there is also a very determined effort on the part of many State boards to bring about the abolition of the small-unit (political) almshouse and to replace it with an organization founded on a unit large enough to make efficient, effective, economical administration feasible.[7]

Discussing the problem from the point of view of the cost of operation, the North Carolina State Board of Charities and Public Welfare, using the first congressional district of the state as an example of what might be done under a district plan, said in 1922:

[6] J. L. Gillin, *Poverty and Dependency*, p. 181.
[7] Estelle M. Stewart, *The Cost of the American Almshouse.* Bulletin of the U. S. Bureau of Labor Statistics, No. 386.

We have a territory with a county home population, taking the average per month for last year, of 89. There are now 77. To care for 80 or 90 people the counties in the district are attempting to maintain twelve institutions. Two others are standing idle. The cost per month per inmate last year varied from $14 in Pasquotank to $89 in Pitt. The average for the district was $38.65 per capita per month as compared with $23.30 for the State Hospital for the Insane at Raleigh. Only one county fell materially below the cost of the State Hospital. Eight went considerably above. Two more than doubled it, and one cost almost four times as much. For one county (Martin) we have been unable to obtain any figures.

The counties of this district have invested in county homes a total of $157,627. Of this amount $71,867 is the total values of buildings. This leaves $85,760 as the total value of farms and farm equipment. The total cost of maintenance for eleven county homes in the district for the year ending November 30, 1921, was $37,011.57.

Suppose these counties should decide to build one institution. They have property on which they should be able to realize at least $100,000 for the central plant. There would have to be some readjustment as to the proportions of the maintenance fund raised by the various counties, but with the total they could meet the following budget:

Superintendent	$ 2,500.00
Matron	1,500.00
Two practical nurses	2,500.00
Physician's services	1,500.00
Board, etc., at $20 per month per inmate	21,360.00
Miscellaneous	1,000.00
Surplus	6,651.57
Total	$37,011.57
Present expenditures for maintenance of eleven county homes	$37,011.57

In selecting a congressional district we do not intend to suggest that the congressional district furnishes the best unit for the district hospital home. We mean merely to suggest that a small number of district homes of a creditable type may be operated at about the same cost as the present large number of county homes.[8]

Continuing the discussion two years later, the Board added:

The Legislature at its 1923 regular session passed a law providing for the forming of districts and the building of district hospital-homes for the aged and infirm. So far no district has been formed under this law. Several counties have discussed the matter, but they have been unable to agree. Usually the trouble has been that the counties could not get together on the location of the institution. Local jealousies must be overcome and local pride sometimes violated if we are to make progress. The Legislature has made it possible for the small county to solve the problem of the county home by coöperation with its neighbors. The district home cannot be located in all of the counties of the district. It cannot be located on neutral ground, because there is no such ground. Concessions must be made. It is a challenge to the efficiency of county government.[9]

The State of Virginia has had better success. She has just succeeded in establishing two consolidated almshouses, one for the eighth congressional district and the other for five counties in the Valley of Virginia. The

[8] North Carolina State Board of Charities and Public Welfare, *Biennial Report, 1920-22*, p. 65.

[9] *Poor Relief in North Carolina*, North Carolina State Board of Charities and Public Welfare. *Special Bulletin No. 4, 1925*, p. 22. The law, which through an error in the office of the Secretary of State was printed as a public-local law, was reënacted by the General Assembly of 1927 (*Public Laws*, chap. 192).

first takes the place of seven county almshouses with a
total inmate population of sixty-two. The second sup-
plants five almshouses with a combined population of
thirty inmates. A third district home is in process of
organization. The State Board of Public Welfare tells of
the accomplishment enthusiastically in a bulletin entitled: *The Disappearance of the County Almshouse in
Virginia: Back from "Over the Hill."*[10]

Virginia has pointed the way for the elimination of
the very small county almshouse. The larger unit will
doubtless make possible an institution maintained in accord with higher standards of physical comfort at the
same cost. But does the larger unit solve the social problems presented by the almshouse? The almshouse system
is indeed "hoary with age, deep-rooted."[11] It traces its
lineage through ages of slow development from the days
when Saxon chieftains ruled their petty kingdoms in England. Customs and attitudes thus slowly established are
hard to overthrow. Numbers of inmates as large as those
in the Virginia consolidated almshouses do not guarantee
a revolution of methods. The Wake County Hospital (as
the county home in Wake County has for several years
been officially designated) has about one hundred twenty-
five inmates. In 1926, when Evans, in *The American Poorfarm and Its Inmates*, charged that in this institution
there was inadequate separation of the sexes and low

[10] Virginia State Board of Public Welfare, *The Disappearance of
the County Almshouse in Virginia.*

[11] Evans, *op. cit.*

morals, and no segregation of the sick, the syphilitic mingling with the well,[12] there was a storm of indignant protest from county officials. They were able to show that the institution had the reputation of being clean and one of the best kept in the state; but it had to be admitted that at least one child recently had been born in the home to an inmate mother. The father was a laborer on the farm. They were able to show that unusual attention was given the sick by the county physician; but the best showing he could make on the syphilis charge was the statement that none of those afflicted were in the infectious stage.[13] There were no adequate facilities for segregating such sick. Is there much reason to suppose that district institutions of the same size under the control of the officials of groups of counties would maintain higher standards?

In 1923 the State Board of Charities and Public Welfare proposed to submit for the consideration of the General Assembly a bill providing for the superseding of the county homes by district hospitals in which there would be a division set aside for the aged and infirm. The proposition failed to meet the approval of the State Board of Health. The bill making possible district almshouses, called in the act *hospital-homes* was submitted instead. What the State Board four years ago suggested with a larger district as the unit it now appears may be feasible in several of the counties on a county basis. It

---

[12] *Ibid.*, p. 67.
[13] *Greensboro Daily News*, August 4, 1926.

may be that the epoch-making step in poor relief in
North Carolina is to be found in the experiment now
being made in Vance County. Here a county home has
been turned into a hospital which meets the requirements
of the Duke Foundation. There is a ward for the aged
and infirm. Good social work has reduced the number of
inmates from twenty-five to seven. Two of these are
regular hospital patients. It has been found practicable
to find care for the others with relatives outside. They
are comfortable and happier than they were in the home,
says the superintendent of public welfare. At the same
time that these former inmates of the county home have
been transferred to the outdoor poor list, the total number
on the list has been reduced one half. The superintendent of the Vance County hospital, including the ward
for the aged and infirm, is a registered nurse. This, it
seems, points the way to a possible solution of the county
almshouse problem in North Carolina, where the Duke
hospital funds are available. Many of the county homes
erected in this state within the last few years might easily
be converted for use as hospitals. Where the county unit
is very small it should be found practicable for two or
more counties to unite to establish a district hospital.
What has been accomplished in Vance County should be
attainable in other counties. The small group of inmates
of the county home might in many cases be made still
smaller by a little intelligent social planning. The remaining inmates, other than those who are legitimate
hospital patients, might have set aside for them a special

ward, as has been done in Vance County. The whole Vance institution is run on hospital standards and, if there were to be any tendency to fall below those standards, it would be held to them by the requirements of the Duke Foundation, from which a large part of its support comes. Wherever such a conversion of the county home into a hospital could be made, there would be a definite and final break with the poorhouse tradition.

SELECTED BIBLIOGRAPHY

Abbott, E., and Breckenridge, S. P., *The Administration of the Aid-to-Mothers Law in Illinois*. Washington, U. S. Children's Bureau, 1921.

Ashe, S. A., *History of North Carolina*. 2 vols. Greensboro, C. L. Van Noppen, 1908.

Ashley, W. J., *An Introduction to English Economic History and Theory*. London, Longmans, Green and Co., 1920.

Bassett, J. S. (ed.), *The Writings of Colonel William Byrd of Westover in Virginia, Esqr.* Garden City, N. Y., Doubleday, Page and Co., 1901.

Brown, R. M., *Poor Relief in North Carolina*. Special Bulletin No. 4. Raleigh, State Board of Charities and Public Welfare, 1925.

Capen, E. W., *The Historical Development of the Poor Laws of Connecticut*. New York, Columbia University Press, 1905.

Carstens, C. C., *Public Pensions to Women and Children*. New York, Russell Sage Foundation, 1913.

Charity Service Reports. Cook County, Illinois, Chicago, 1924.

Colonial Records of North Carolina (ed. W. L. Saunders). Raleigh, P. M. Hale, Printer to the State, 1886-90.

Cummings, John, *Poor Laws of Massachusetts and New York*. New York, The Macmillan Co., 1895.

Disappearance of the County Almshouse in Virginia, The. Richmond, Virginia State Board of Public Welfare, 1926.

Dix, D. L., *Memorial . . . to the General Assembly of North Carolina, 1848*. House of Commons Document, No. 2. Raleigh, Seaton Gales, 1848.

Ellwood, C. A., *Conditions of the County Almshouses of Missouri*. The University of Missouri, Columbia, Mo., 1904.

Evans, H. C., *The American Poorfarm and Its Inmates*. Des Moines, Loyal Order of the Moose, 1926.

Folkes, Homer, *The Care of Destitute, Neglected and Delinquent Children*. New York, The Macmillan Co., 1902.

Frankel, E., *Poor Relief in Pennsylvania*. Harrisburg, State Department of Public Welfare, 1925.

Gillin, J. L., *History of Poor Relief Legislation in Iowa*. Iowa City, State Historical Society of Iowa, 1914.

———— *Poverty and Dependency* (rev. ed.). New York, The Century Co., 1925.

Grimes, J. B., *Notes on Colonial North Carolina, 1700-1750*. Raleigh, North Carolina Historical Commission, 1905.

Heffner, W. C., *History of Poor Relief Legislation in Pennsylvania*. Cleon, Penna., Holzaphel, 1913.

Hinrichsen, Annie, *The District Almshouse for Illinois*. Proceedings of the National Conference of Social Work, 1918.

Johnson, Alexander, *Adventures in Social Welfare, Fort Wayne, Indiana*. Fort Wayne Publishing Co., 1923.

———— *The Almshouse, Construction and Management*. New York, Charities Publication Committee, 1911.

Kelso, R. W., *History of Public Poor Relief in Massachusetts, 1620-1920*. Boston, Houghton Mifflin Co., 1922.

Lawson, John, *History of North Carolina*, being a reprint of the copy now in the North Carolina State Library, Raleigh, etc. Charlotte, 1903.

McLean, F. H., *The Poor and Alms Department and the Almshouse of Newark, New Jersey*. New York, Russell Sage Foundation, 1913.

Manual of the Mother's Assistance Fund. Harrisburg, Penna., Pennsylvania Department of Public Welfare, 1922.

Nesbitt, F., *Standards of Public Aid to Children in Their Own Homes*. Washington, U. S. Children's Bureau, 1923.

New Jersey Special Commission Report. Trenton, 1923.

Nicholls, Sir George, *History of the English Poor Law*. 2 vols. New York, G. P. Putnam's Sons, 1918.

North Carolina Legislative Documents, 1872-73. Document No. 22.

North Carolina State Board of Charities and Public Welfare, *Biennial Report, 1920-22; Biennial Report, 1922-24; Biennial Report, 1924-26.*

North Carolina State Board of Public Charities, *Report, 1870; Report, 1872.*

Paupers in Almshouses. Washington, U. S. Bureau of the Census, 1924.

"Poor Law," *Encyclopaedia Britannica.*

Queen, S. A., *Social Work in the Light of History.* Philadelphia, J. B. Lippincott Co., 1922.

Rathbone, E. F., *The Disinherited Family* (3rd ed.). New York, Longmans, Green and Co., 1927.

Report of the Mother's Assistance Fund, Harrisburg, Penna., Pennsylvania Department of Public Welfare, 1924.

Shotwell, Mary G., *The Care of Dependent Children in Institutions.* Special Bulletin No. 5. Raleigh, State Board of Charities and Public Welfare, 1925.

State Records of North Carolina (ed. Walter Clark). Goldsboro, N. C., Nash Brothers, 1886-1907.

Stewart, Estelle M., *The Cost of the American Almshouse.* Washington, U. S. Bureau of Labor Statistics, 1925.

Summary of State Laws Relating to Public Aid to Children in Their Own Homes. Washington, U. S. Children's Bureau, 1925.

Tuttle, Emeth, *Mothers' Aid in North Carolina.* Special Bulletin No. 7. Raleigh, State Board of Charities and Public Welfare, 1926.

Warfield, G. A., and Riley, T. J., *Outdoor Relief in Missouri.* New York, Survey Associates, Inc., 1915.

Warner, A. G., *American Charities.* New York, Thomas Y. Crowell, 1918.

INDEX

Alamance County, 88, 102, 109

Almshouse, 5, 28, 29, 32, 40, 57-66, 72-89, 163
—admission to, 28, 29, 48
—combined with jail, 61
—conditions in, 89-92
—cost of maintenance, 47, 77, 85-94, 121, 123-25
—designated "county home," 70
—discipline in, 53
—disinfectants, use in, 107
—district, 165-71
—equipment of, 104-6
—food furnished inmates, 79-80, 86, 87, 130-31
—inmates, 49-53, 72-73, 82-83, 103
—location of, 103
—McDonald report, 101
—marriage of inmates, 78
—medical attention in, 64, 65, 77, 28-30, 164-65
—necessary expense, 70
—Pasquotank, opened, 40
—prisoners in, 98
—records in, 131
—report of 1920, 101
—sanitation in, 60, 76, 90, 93, 106-8
—superintendent, appointment of, 57, 69
—supervision of, 80-81, 93, 119, 113-22
—survey of 1922, 101-2
—system, lack of, 90
—types of, 74-75, 77, 82-83, 85, 92, 102, 115

Apprenticeship, 6, 7, 22, 147, 150

Bastards, 6, 13, 14, 35, 38, 149

Beaufort County, 64, 88, 108
Bennehan, Thomas D., Will of, 48
Berry, Charles, 149
Blacknall, G. W., 72, 73
Bladen County, 75
Blind, care of, 94
Board of State Charities, 71
Brunswick County, 31, 124
Buncombe County, 61, 74, 82, 86, 102
Bureau of Mental Hygiene and Health, 126
Burke County, 61, 102, 118
Byrd, William, 1, 16

Cabarrus County, 62, 86
Caldwell County, 102
Carson, Matthew, 42
Carteret County, 28, 29, 108
Caswell County, 29, 59, 102
Caswell Training School, 125
Chain gang, 97
Charities and Public Welfare, county boards of. See County boards.
Charities and Public Welfare, State Board of. See State Board of Charities and Public Welfare.
Charities, State Board of Public. See State Board of Public Charities.
Chatham County, 28, 83, 88, 102, 109
Cherokee County, 102, 139
Child, Thomas, 149
Child-placing, 6, 7, 22, 146-50, 154-56
Children:
—apprenticing of, 6, 7, 22, 146-50
—blind, 94-95, 156
—born in almshouses, 116, 117, 127-28

State Board of Charities and
Public Welfare, 100, 115, 125,
126
State sanatorium for tuberculosis, 96
St. Gabriel's Parish, minutes
of, 37-39
St. John's College, 152
Stokes County, 59
Strudwick, E., 44, 45
Superintendent of almshouse:
—appointment of, 57
—education of, 118
—immoral relations with inmates, 78
—occupation, farmer, 118-19
—salary, 75, 85, 113
—types of, 77, 80, 87, 109
Superintendents of public welfare, 100, 119-22, 133-45
Surry County, 29, 60, 111, 124

Tax for support of poor, 7,
20, 21, 26, 27, 28, 31, 35, 47,
67, 69
Testerman, Jasper 42
Thomas, Ann, 14
Thomasville Orphanage, 159
Transylvania County, 74
Tuberculosis sanatorium, 96
Turner, Josiah, 44, 54
Tyrrell County, 88, 108

Urmstone, John, 14-15
United States Bureau of Labor
Statistics, 167

Vance County, 102, 109, 120-
22, 140
Vance County hospital, 172-73
Vegetable gardens, 80, 91, 112
Virginia:
—citizens pasturing stock in
Currituck County, 36

—complaints as to runaway
slaves and servants, 16
—district almshouses, 169
—visitors, county boards of,
83

Wake County, 29, 83, 85, 88,
102, 165, 170
Wardens of the poor, 26, 27, 31,
35, 37, 53, 66:
—admission to poorhouse by,
29, 39
—abuse of powers by, 56-57
—build almshouses, 28, 29,
31, 67
—employ superintendent of
poorhouse, 34
—exploitation of poor by, 56
—levy tax, 67
—method of selection, 53,
66-67
—oath of office, 43
—records of, 37-54
—type of men, 53-54
—wardens of Ashe County, 42
—wardens of Orange County,
42
Warren County, 29
Watauga County, 74, 88, 92,
102, 116, 124
Watts, Thomas D., 42, 43
Wayne County, 28, 64, 102
Weaver, William, 42
Webb, James, 42, 52
Welker, G. W., 71, 72, 76
Western counties, 76
Wilkes County, 61
Wilson County, 102, 108
Woman, legal settlement of, 35
Workhouse, 32, 33, 34, 83, 97
"Workhouse test," 8, 139

Yadkin County, 85
Yancey County, 74, 108

www.ingramcontent.com/pod-product-compliance
Lightning Source LLC
Chambersburg PA
CBHW030649270326
41929CB00007B/275